THE SURGE OF PIETY IN AMERICA

THE SURGE OF PIETY

IN AMERICA

AN APPRAISAL

By A. Roy Eckardt

ASSOCIATION PRESS • NEW YORK

*To My Mother
and Father*
ANNA F. ECKARDT
FREDERICK W. ECKARDT
*Whose honor
is piety,
but not new*

Acknowledgments

The following are among the many publishers and authors who have kindly consented to the use of copyrighted material:

The Christian Century Foundation, Chicago—Selected editorials and articles copyright 1955 and 1957, reprinted by permission from *The Christian Century*.

Doubleday & Company, Inc., Garden City, New York— *Peace with God* by Billy Graham, copyright 1953 by Billy Graham; *Protestant-Catholic-Jew* by Will Herberg, copyright 1955 by Will Herberg, reprinted by permission.

Harvard University Press, Cambridge, Massachusetts— *Religion in 20th Century America* by Herbert W. Schneider, copyright 1952 by The President and Fellows of Harvard College, reprinted by permission of the publishers.

Thomas Nelson & Sons, New York—*The Revised Standard*

Version of the Holy Bible, copyright 1946 and 1952 by the National Council of the Churches of Christ in the U.S.A., used by permission.

Prentice-Hall, Inc., Englewood Cliffs, New Jersey—*Stay Alive All Your Life* by Norman Vincent Peale, copyright 1957 by Prentice-Hall, Inc., published by Prentice-Hall, Inc., Englewood Cliffs, New Jersey.

This Week Magazine, New York—"Why I Believe in the Devil" by Billy Graham, copyright 1958 by the United Newspapers Magazine Corporation.

The Westminster Press, Philadelphia—*Protestantism in America* by Jerald C. Brauer, copyright 1953 by W. L. Jenkins, The Westminster Press, used by permission.

Other publishers by whom permission has been granted for the use of excerpts, but who do not require exact credit lines, are credited in footnotes to the main text at the end of each chapter. Grateful acknowledgment for these courtesies is here expressed.

A hill *ca'n't* be a valley, you know.
That would be nonsense. . . .
Alice in *Through the
Looking-Glass*

Every valley shall be lifted up, and
every mountain and hill be made low.
Isaiah 40:4 (RSV)

Preface

Several years ago *The Christian Century* published an article of mine on the subject of America's "turn to religion" ("The New Look in American Piety," November 17, 1954). What began as rather incidental, though disturbed, musing on my part has turned into continuing and, I trust, a little less captious reflection. However, the present study is written from a predominantly critical point of view. Although a number of passages report or reflect the contentions of other people, I do considerable evaluating on my own. And there is much polemic here. Further, I make no claim to exhaustiveness. The study as a whole is rather impressionistic. It is intended, primarily, to be suggestive.

Inclusion of a list of those who have read and criticized an author's manuscript is a time-honored device. Part of its effect may be to shake the reader's self-confidence and upset his critical faculties. In trying to frame objections, he cannot quite get out of his consciousness the many people—often "very important people"—who have gone

11

before him and, on the surface at least, provided a stamp of some kind of approval. I have made no effort to supply such a list here. I am aware that this deficiency represents a serious breach of literary etiquette. The one consolation is that I have no one to whom I can shift the blame—except, of course, to myself.

My wife, Alice Lyons Eckardt, has performed a valued service, not in the role of scapegoat but in that of indispensable helpmate. She graciously assumed the onerous but crucial task of helping me to overcome the many shortcomings of a first draft, faults which Mr. James Rietmulder, Director of Association Press, had previously exposed with fitting candor. The defects that remain are mine.

A. ROY ECKARDT

Lehigh University
Bethlehem, Pennsylvania

Contents

Acknowledgments   7

Preface   11

Introduction   17

ONE: The Recent "Turn to Religion" and the
      Problem of Its Roots   21

*Institutional Growth. Piety Everywhere. A Time
of Troubles. Religion in General and Religion
in Particular. Religiousness Amidst Secularity.
Protestant-Catholic-Jew. Piety Anywhere.*

TWO: Folk Religion: Its Ways and Works   42

*Folk Religion and Culture Religion. The Mean-
ing of Folk Religion. Focus on the Individual.
Focus on Society. The Theology of Folk Reli-*

13

*gion. Folk Religion and Billy Graham. Ameri-
can Backgrounds. The Domestication of Faith.
Folk Religion Through the Back Door. The
Attractions of Folk Religion.*

THREE: An Irreverent Intrusion: Ironic Hazards in
      the New Religion   68

      *The Elusiveness of Motivation. The Meaning
      of Irony. Intellectuals and the Simple Life.*

FOUR: Ironic Strains in "The Cult of Reassurance"   73

      *The New Anxiety. The High Priest of the Cult.
      Freedom, Fate, and a Final Formula. The Call
      to Self-Centeredness and Success.*

FIVE: Irony and the Revival of Revivalism   93

      *The Evangelist and the Holy Adversary. At-
      traction and Repulsion. An Easy Answer. The
      New Fundamentalism. Revivalism and the
      Church. The Futility of It All.*

SIX: Irony and the Gospel of Group Interest   119

      *A Mutual Admiration Society. The Nemesis of
      Patriotic Piety. Matter, Spirit, and Responsi-
      bility. Variations on the Theme of Idolatry.
      "Free Enterprise," Human and Divine. "The
      American Way" and the American Tradition.
      Man the Measure.*

SEVEN: Irony, Conformity, and Conformism   135

      *Conformist Temptations. We Organization
      Men. Conformism and the New Piety. Enter
      the Church.*

EIGHT: In Search of a Christian Stand   153

Wheels Within Wheels. Physician, Judge Thyself. The Ways That Are Not Our Ways. The Truth That May Find Us. No Axe to Grind for Religion. Utility Versus Purity. Our New Gospels, the Social Gospel, and the Whole Gospel. On the Resolution of Human Problems. A Summary Reckoning. Disputation Taken Captive By Love.

Index   189

Introduction

The purpose of this study is to assay in brief form a few recent tendencies in our religious life. In the course of the past decade and more, visible, substantial, and fairly rapid change has taken place in the American religious scene. The possible significance of this observation is tempered somewhat by the fact that American life as a whole has always been a highly dynamic affair. Nevertheless, if overt evidence is any guide, our nation has been experiencing of late a considerable intensification of religiousness or at least of religiosity.

We should hardly say that a great "religious revival" has been under way in the United States. The most that can be asserted, with the support of many competent observers, is that we have witnessed a manifest upsurge of *interest* in religion.

No pretense is made here of dealing with any "main direction" of contemporary American religion as a whole. To insist that there is just a single direction would be a highly risky exercise—until, perhaps, future historians may be able to identify the direction and thus vindicate the claim. There is much more to the religious life and thinking of Americans than the tendencies here chosen for emphasis. Little will be said about the forms and expressions of American religion which preceded these tendencies— forms and expressions which continue to be active and which will doubtless outlast the recent surge of piety. Neither does the contemporary intellectual renewal of interest in religion enter the discussion, other than in an oblique way.

Emphasis will fall on description and appraisal of certain popular forms of religion, of which Norman Vincent Peale and Billy Graham are conspicuous representatives. If we refer a number of times to these two men, it is not because without them there would be nobody to talk about; it is, on the contrary, because of a conviction that the wideness of their followings reveals much about contemporary American religion. They are symptoms as well as leaders.

There is a distinct possibility that social autosuggestion may be at work in the new discussion of things religious. A curious thing about human ideology as a whole is the way men are able to talk themselves into a measure of social change. Few things have been more fashionable of late than pointing out how religion has become very fashionable. If enough people get together and agree that something noteworthy is taking place, and if they succeed in securing a sufficient social hearing, the first thing we know, the idea they have conjured up may begin to materialize. This is the more likely since mass communication has come. And it holds especially where the society is, in David Riesman's phrase, largely "other-directed." We live in a time when many people anxiously watch their peers

for signals of what to do and say next. This is not to insinuate that the appearance of this small book will change
any course of events. Yet, in saying our piece, we may,
embarrassingly, contribute in some slight way to the con-
juring habit. It is apparent, however, that the face of
American religion was already undergoing noteworthy
change before the "eggheads"—professors, clergy, social
critics, and the like—could break into print with their
words of wisdom and confusion. The phenomena before
us are sufficiently objective and evident that we are justified in talking about them and reacting to them.

It would be foolish to assert that the changes in question will abide forever. There are, indeed, some signs that
the crest of the recent flood of religious interest may already have passed. At this writing, the new piety is becoming a little old. It is not quite so vocal or manifest as it
was as recently as one or two years ago. This is one reason
the word "surge" is used in the title of the book. The
term suggests a sudden rising, but one that is inevitably
followed by a falling, as the waves of the sea. What will
happen in the next few years is, of course, anyone's guess.

Our usage of the term "piety" also requires clarification. This word often connotes something praiseworthy,
as when people refer to "pious souls" in contrast to impious or worldly men. However, from the point of view of
the present study, piety is not to be construed as something that necessarily warrants moral and spiritual approval. In the pages that follow, piety is conceived within
the context of "folk religion," a form of American religious life which is explicated in Chapter Two and evaluated critically all through the study.

We do not claim to be able either to understand fully
the American "turn to religion" or to place that develop-

ment within a final framework of explanation. If, as Arthur M. Schlesinger, Jr., writes in *The Crisis of the Old Order,* "we are always in a zone of imperfect visibility so far as the history just over our shoulder is concerned," it follows that our vision approaches zero when we seek to understand events happening before our eyes. On the other hand, the new piety has probably been with us long enough to justify exploratory analysis and appraisal.

Chapter : O N E

The Recent "Turn to Religion" and the
Problem of Its Roots

It is not necessary to adduce arguments in support of the observation that there has been a nation-wide "turn to religion" in the United States. Illustrations are sufficient, and these simply underline facts that everyone knows.

Institutional Growth

Within the precincts of the churches and other religious institutions of a traditional sort, including to a certain extent the immediate family, the propriety of overt religious expression has, of course, always been maintained. Yet, traditional religion itself has been substantially involved in the recent upsurge in activity. That this is so reflects considerable support by secular society. Institutional religion may grow as much by the faith it proclaims as by the social status it manages to achieve. But the latter is always there—in a way that at once indicates social approval and justifies sociological interpretation.

The ultimate meaning and value of statistics remains an enigma for social analysis. For their possible worth here are officially reported figures on the changing proportions of American "church members" (of all faiths) to the total population during the past century:

$$
\begin{array}{ll}
1850 & 16.0\% \\
1860 & 23.0\% \\
1870 & 18.0\% \\
1880 & 20.0\% \\
1890 & 22.0\% \\
1900 & 36.0\% \\
1910 & 43.0\% \\
1920 & 43.0\% \\
1930 & 47.0\% \\
1940 & 49.0\% \\
1950 & 57.0\% \\
1954 & 60.3\% \\
1955 & 60.9\% \\
1956 & 62.0\% \; *\,1
\end{array}
$$

In addition to the fact that church statistics are notoriously unreliable, only one certain conclusion can be drawn from these figures: There has been a tendency toward increasing institutionalization in American religion. In themselves the figures convey no information respecting the strength of religious faith. It is the case that all through the history of this country the proportion of church members within the total population has risen. On the other hand, percentages of church membership have increased at a conspicuously more rapid rate since 1940 than in the course of the preceding two decades. The

* All footnotes appear at the ends of chapters.

number of church members of all faiths grew from 54,576,346 in 1926 to 86,830,490 in 1950 to 103,224,954 in 1956.[2]

Comparable figures are available on such items as church attendance, financial support, enrollments in Sunday and Sabbath schools, and the construction of new religious buildings.[3]

Piety Everywhere

We have recently witnessed a diffusion of piety in ways that widely supplement the regular ministries of the churches. Piety has proliferated beyond the bounds of traditional institutional effort into many areas of American life. It has penetrated into politics. Prayer has always been offered in the halls of Congress as well as in lesser legislative bodies. Chaplains have ministered to the Armed Forces. But the bond between religion and political life has been noticeably strengthened by recent developments. William Lee Miller has referred to our national "piety along the Potomac," involving Bible breakfasts, special church services, congressional prayer groups, a red, white, and blue postage stamp rivaling our coins with its motto, "In God We Trust," and the addition of the words "under God" to the Pledge of Allegiance.[4] More recently, "In God We Trust" has taken its place on our folding money as well. Beyond these things, Congress has now set aside a "meditation room" in the Capitol for its own private use.

But perhaps the most significant indication of a new positive relation between religion and politics is the continued reference to religion and the churches by political figures. It is almost impossible to imagine a candidate for high—or even low—office bringing up probing questions concerning the worth of religion without at the same time running the risk of political suicide. To give voice to such thoughts would be like raising public doubts about the sanctity of the home or the value of integrity. Such explicit alliance of the political with the religious life, particularly religious institutional life, has not always prevailed in American history.

Our surging piety has also made itself at home in the world of entertainment. One conspicuous area is popular music. To follow the Hit Parade is to be reminded of the word of Job, "He shall hold it fast, but it shall not endure." Yet, if last year's crop of hit songs centering in religious themes has already begun to gather dust, others may be on hand before too long to grace the racks in the music shops and to sound forth from the juke boxes. In addition, the movie makers have long since learned that extravaganzas with religious themes possess inspired appeal at the box office.

Politics and entertainment are but two illustrations among many others. Articles and books "of a religious and inspirational nature" have gained a prominent place in secular and commercial publishing. Religious events receive wide and sympathetic coverage in periodicals and newspapers. Printed forms with alternate graces for Protestants, Catholics, and Jews vie with the menus and wine lists in restaurants and dining cars. In at least one football conference and probably more, games are started with prayer. Radio and TV stations pause not simply for the usual station breaks but for reminding their listeners to "go to church on Sunday." The "Religion in American Life" campaign, directed by a layman's committee with support from the Advertising Council of America, receives gratis some $6 million worth of advertising in a number of media for promoting its objective, which is "to emphasize the importance of all religious institutions as the foundations of American life and to urge all Americans to attend and support the church or synagogue of their individual choice."

All this piety hardly involves a total contrast in kind with every other period of American life. The historian will doubtless discern similarities—as well as differences—with earlier epochs. The only explicit contrast to be made here is with the America in which many of the readers of this book were raised. It is a contrast of significant degree. In the passing generation the agnostic and the skeptic were not lacking in social recognition. Today there is a suspicion in the air that it is somehow un-American to be an atheist—or at least to talk up atheism publicly. The "negative dogmatisms" of atheism and skepticism have become considerably less acceptable. The religionist, by contrast, can anticipate increasing social approval. Even the dogmatic religionist tends to be granted a respectful hearing. Religion may involve certain secrets of the soul. Yet, it has become quite proper to exhibit one's spiritual inclinations openly.

Religion has come into vogue. It is very much at home among Americans. All this is obvious. But why the vogue? The issue of the ultimate inspiration of the "turn to religion" involves us in extremely difficult questions. It is not here claimed that a fully satisfactory explanation can be developed. We are dealing with a highly complex and rather amorphous social phenomenon. A search for the roots of our surging piety may, however, contribute something to our understanding of the phenomenon itself.

A Time of Troubles

A prevailing mode of explanation will serve as a point of departure. Many interpreters emphasize the peculiar pressures of the times. We include this general interpretation not only because it is very widespread but because, as we shall see, it typifies the perplexities that any analyst faces.

Emphasis may be placed on the fact that there are many spiritually displaced persons in the modern world.[5] The religious spirit in man abhors a vacuum. Countless people no longer subscribe to the faith of their fathers. Recent alternatives to that faith, such as social reformism and science, have been revealed as illusory saviors. Hence, many persons, groping for a spiritual home, have been attracted by new forms of piety, particularly of the "peace of mind" and "peace of soul" varieties. These solutions usually contain carry-overs from traditional Christian faith—at least they include some of the old symbols and language—in combination with elements taken over from the insights of modern psychology.

Ronald Gregor Smith is somewhat more specific:

You might expect that modern man, who has such immense successes to his credit in opening up his world, would calmly recognise that he is the captain of his soul and the master of his fate. You might expect him to cultivate his garden in peace, to play his part in the great world and to relinquish his part when the time comes with only a little sigh for its transience. But it is not like that at all. On the contrary, individual modern man is distressed and perplexed. He feels his helplessness in the great world and he feels his helplessness in his private inner world.[6]

These remarks were addressed to a British audience. But "modern man" is of many nationalities. Wherever he is, he may conceivably turn to religion for an answer to his helplessness—although this scarcely accounts for the sort of religion that emphasizes human powers. Indeed, the fact that men persist in seeking an answer to their plight goes to show that they have hardly given themselves up.

Herbert W. Schneider also stresses the troubles of the times but gives particular attention to the terrible cruelty modern man has experienced.

In the face of such cruelty man is also immediately face to face with God; he does not need to seek God, but finds himself driven to God. This means in the language of Santayana, that "piety" takes precedence over "spirituality"; that basic human loyalties are being tested so severely that the positive efforts in the pursuit of happiness and other ideals are pushed into the background. The problem of *facing* evil (internally and externally) is real to us, over and above the problem of *abolishing* evil. Americans were especially unprepared spiritually for this turn of events, having imagined the twentieth century to be naturally destined to be "the century of progress." [7]

Shortly before his death, Paul Hutchinson wrote an article in *Life* appraising the new religious trend. Hutchinson maintained that "it is among us middle-brows" that the "phenomenon of an American religious stirring is most striking." Since this group comprises the most influential segment of American life, the significance of the religious stirring is thereby enhanced. Although middle-brow piety takes many forms, its influence on the public consciousness is made most profoundly, according to Hutchinson, through "the cult of reassurance." This cult is described as a flocking to religion, especially in middle-class circles, for a renewal of confidence and optimism at a time when these are in short supply. It is a turning to the priest for encouragement to believe that, despite everything that has happened in this dismaying century, the world is good, life is good, the human story makes sense and comes out where we want it to come out.[8]

Men have always turned to their gods for an answer to worry and failure and as a means of securing rewards for their assumed righteousness. What we are witnessing today, Hutchinson claimed, is a new form of solution to the age-old quest for happiness and a satisfying life. We see before us a cult of affirmation which rejects outright various contemporary cults of denial. The country is full of people who find themselves hard put to say what is wrong with them but who are nevertheless confused, frustrated, and depressed. They embody the loss of nerve which is so characteristic of our time. The great response to the cult of reassurance is a measure of the universal human hunger for hope.

Social critics sometimes portray people as more despondent and perplexed than they really are. In this connection, it appears that the general populace tends to react somewhat more quickly to immediate changes in the fortunes of the times than does the more philosophic intellectual—rather especially, it seems, when the signs are on the bright side. This is the second decade since Hiroshima and Nagasaki; and somehow the Bomb, while greatly swollen in size, has not fallen again. At this writing (*sic!*), the American economy, although under noticeable strain, is apparently not in danger of collapse. And now the conquest of space has all at once appeared on the horizon, with its promise of an intriguing future. Generally speaking, the current observer who paints a picture of people ridden with anxiety, tension, and hopelessness wields too heavy a brush. Schneider's assertion that "basic human loyalties are being tested so severely that the positive efforts in the pursuit of happiness and other ideals are pushed into the background" illustrates this artificiality of judgment. In actuality, the pursuit of happiness is a going concern in contemporary America. Paul Hutchinson's analysis is, of course, exempt from this criticism. For him, the new religion may have been sown in the soil of despair all right, but it is the undefeated human spirit that makes possible the fruits.

In March of 1952, the same year that Schneider's study appeared, George Gallup polled a cross section of the American people on the question, "As you look to the future, do you think life for people generally will get better—or will it get worse?" The results follow:

Better......................42%
Worse......................34%
Same.......................13%
Don't know................11%

As Gallup commented at the time, the figures apparently indicate that in spite of such conditions as high taxes, inflation, and the threat of war, optimism remains the prevailing note among the American people. Despite the initial shock caused by Soviet missile and satellite advances, in all probability results rather similar to Gallup's findings would be forthcoming if another such poll were taken at the present time. Probably the most accurate judgment is that American anxieties about life and the future are balanced by continuing faith in humanity.

To be sure, human anxieties may be merely repressed

rather than overcome. It is the case that men are never spared the apprehension which accompanies living on the edge of an abyss—the abyss of hardship, suffering, and death. But all this is nothing new in human experience. The American surge of piety may have arisen in part out of the crisis of the times, but it is doubtful whether that state of affairs is the one fundamental cause. This is not to neglect the background consideration that ours is an epoch in which many of the foundations of traditional culture are lost and there is much human dislocation and uncertainty.[9]

Under the next heading of this chapter a more basic difficulty is seen in the view which traces the new American piety to our time of troubles.

Religion in General and Religion in Particular

Attempts to account for overt social tendencies such as the general religious development under present discussion tend to be variations within two main types. Now universal elements are emphasized, and now particular factors are accentuated. From the former point of view, religion is manifested again and again within different societies as the representation of a general human condition. Thus, stress may fall upon the fact that man as such is a finite being, living an uncertain—although in many ways joyful—existence and, with it all, aware in the depths of his being that he and his world are not all they might be or ought to become. It appears to be essential to man as man that he search for and find some divinely grounded rationale for the puzzle and the pain, and some divine benefactor from whom he may secure pardon and power and to whom he may render thanks.

From another point of view, man is seen in his particularity. Inevitably, specific forms of human experience develop as part and parcel of certain societies and certain epochs. Hence, religious life will take form and find meaning only through concrete historical situations. In following out the logic of this approach, some may conclude that a given manifestation of religiousness arises, more or less fortuitously, from out of a conglomeration of particular occurrences, such as one or more inventions or a series of decisive events or the appearance of certain dominant personalities. To let our imaginations have free play for a moment, suppose that the last quarter of a century had seen *none* of these: the phenomenal development of mass communication, World War II, the Bomb, and the careers of Fulton J. Sheen, Norman Vincent Peale, and Billy Graham. Would we have experienced a revival of interest in religion anything like the recent one? To interject that other influential factors and people would have probably come along in no way annuls the theory; it may, indeed, simply underscore it.

Corresponding to the explanatory tendencies above are two difficulties which, from opposite quarters, confront any attempt to disclose the roots of the upsurge in American piety. The spokesman for a generalized orientation is tempted to treat a particular manifestation of religiousness exclusively from the standpoint of religion as a universal phenomenon. With somewhat less abstractness, the interpreter may concentrate, in effect, upon the alleged religiousness of "twentieth-century man." In neither case does the analyst come to grips with the contemporary American scene as the required focus of interpretation.

The opposite danger is to become so specific and partial that the interpreter mistakes surface developments for roots, failing to surmount the passing phase. Thus, he may concentrate so much upon particular events and particular leaders that he loses sight of the unavoidable question of what are the fundamental and prevenient conditions which permit particular factors to exert such significant social influence. In this connection, it is always extremely difficult to estimate reliably the extent of the originating and continuing effect that given events and persons will have—until, at least, a good many years have elapsed.

Occasionally the two dangers to which we refer appear together. Attention is paid to a present state of affairs of relatively limited scope, but the situation is finally construed from the perspective of fairly generalized and perennial concerns or needs. Thus, the new piety in America is sometimes interpreted as a specific revelation of widespread hunger among men today for the Christian gospel, a gospel which they already dimly recognize but yearn to be grasped by in its saving fullness.

An issue that must give us pause here is that of contemporary resemblances and differences between the state of affairs in which Americans live and that in which other peoples live. It has to be granted that in principle, widely disparate developments as between countries may actually stem from similar or even identical causes. Where, for example, there is world-wide anxiety due to the threat of the catastrophic annihilation of mankind, human beings in general might very well "turn" to religion for aid and comfort. This incentive would then appear to account for the American "turn to religion." Conceivably, men in other lands could be trying to cope with their anxieties in other than consciously or explicitly religious ways.

The difficulty is that this approach simply throws no

light on the question of why *America* should manifest a unique upsurge in religion. The analyst may have merely fallen into provincialism in interpretation. If it is insisted that hunger for the Christian gospel may, after all, be considered in some way universal, the trouble is that, on the one hand, the new American religious interest has not found significant parallels in other lands and, on the other hand, in various parts of the world the Christian cause is in serious difficulties or, as in Great Britain, subject to marked indifference. To be sure, inner spiritual hunger is not necessarily in correlation with the external fortunes of the Christian church; but, once emphasis is placed upon our troublous times, the interpreter must continue to come to terms with specific objective situations.

The general theory which stresses the tragic perplexities of our times doubtless contains some elements of truth. Nevertheless, we are not relieved of searching for factors which in their concreteness transcend common human problems and yet direct us to distinctive elements within the American situation.[10]

Religiousness Amidst Secularity

It is with this continuing task in mind that we refer to the interpretation offered by Will Herberg in a recent study, *Protestant-Catholic-Jew*. Though fully cognizant of the universal human proclivity to religion, Herberg concentrates upon the American scene. For his point of departure he refers to the curious but evident paradox of accelerating secularism amidst mounting religiosity in American life. We cannot brush aside the new religiousness as escapist or artificial or insincere. The real problem of the current religious situation is the secularism of a religious people, or strong religiousness in a profoundly secularist framework.

Herberg's general thesis is that

both the religiousness and the secularism of the American people derive from very much the same sources, and . . . both become more intelligible when seen against the background of certain deep-going sociological processes that have transformed the face of the American people in the course of the past generation.[11]

Herberg emphasizes that for the most part, Americans today are in a real sense third-generation immigrants, statistically but also in their social outlook and way of life. The first immigrant generation was able to conserve most of its ethnic inheritance, but the forces of cultural assimilation exerted powerful influence on the second generation. That generation tended to throw off its inherited religion along with its ethnic inheritance. The trouble, however, is that assimilation threatens self-identity. A man asks, "What am I?", and it is not enough to answer, "I am an American." Americanism is too inchoate to provide the secure resting place and sustenance that human life as a whole demands. Further, our varied ethnic inheritance is just about irrecoverable—save for one crucial strand within it: the religion of our fathers. America is committed to a variety and plurality of religions. The religious views and loyalties of the fathers are wider than the ethnic inheritance or the ethnic group, but they are thought to be consistent with American ideals and they have become identified with "the American Way of Life." In addition, continuing ethnic concerns have been preserved and expressed through the total religious community.

Protestant-Catholic-Jew

And so, Herberg affirms, the third-generation American comes to find his identity either as Protestant or Catholic or Jew—not by external pressure but by inner necessity.[12]

The old image of America as a single melting pot has proved inappropriate. What we actually have is a triple melting pot, or, as Herberg prefers to say, "transmuting pot," since within each of the religious communities what comes out is a "new man" cast and recast along the lines of a common American ideal type. The three major religious communities are viewed as distinguishable representations of such "spiritual values" as the fatherhood of God, the brotherhood of man, and the dignity of the individual for which American democracy is supposed to stand. The three faiths attain equal footing as "the religions of democracy" (to use the revealing title of another book on these faiths). This amounts to what the present writer would describe as the holy trinity of American popular piety—Protestantism, Catholicism, and Judaism.[13] Our total religious picture is a typically American spectacle of the sort that, in one of history's little jokes, so often dazzles the native European who comes to these shores from the very continent that gave birth to the strange young child. Religion functions in a way that provides people with self-identity and social location in the particular historical situation which is modern America. All this helps to make somewhat more understandable how an American revival of religion can be quite compatible with growing secularity.

The peculiar needs and influence of the third generation could have had nothing to do, of course, with per-

centages of church membership during the last century.
Yet, the Herberg thesis may throw considerable light upon
the notable upsurge in more recent years. It was not until
the turn of the century that the curve of church membership moved sharply upward. The trend could reach a
climax in the midtwentieth century because it was then
that the third generation, so to speak, came of age.

Herberg's interpretation is not beyond all criticism. It
leaves certain questions unresolved—for example, the question of the extent to which Negroes and Jews show consistency with the development the author traces.[14] Herberg does seek to take into consideration the special issues
that such groups pose.

The restructuring of American society appears to be
a major factor in the "turn to religion." However, this
national accent upon Protestantism, Catholicism, and
Judaism in terms of a triple melting pot is not the only
possible explanation of the surge of American piety. As
is clear from certain of the illustrations included early in
this chapter, the new religion does not always explicitly
take one of the three major institutional forms.

Herberg does not seek to put across one all-encompass-
ing explanation. He allows for at least three factors beyond
the first one just considered. His second point is the
change in American character structure which David Riesman has emphasized. Until fairly recently American society was prevailingly "inner-directed." The inner-directed
individual is the man who stands on his own two feet,
guided and inspired by powerful drives coming from
within. Of late we have, by contrast, become much more
"other-directed," deriving our standards and goals from
the group and concerning ourselves with adjustment more
than achievement. From this point of view, the turn to

religion partly reflects "the growing other-directedness of our middle-class culture." Church membership can be a symptom of conformity and a promoter of belonging-ness.[15]

Third, Herberg sees considerable truth in the view we referred to above that the contemporary crisis of our whole civilization may drive men to religion. Religion provides peace of mind for the individual and spiritual strength for the nation amidst international strife and uncertainty. Fourth, as something of a reaction to social conformity and to "the erosions of a mass culture," individual Americans may again be turning to an inner religion which serves as "an inexpugnable citadel for the self in a world in which personal authenticity is threatened on every side. "

The desirability of steering a middle course between too generalized and too partial approaches is met in Herberg's first and major interpretation and also in the second. The fourth, in so far as it points to specific reactions to other-directedness on the part of some Americans, is more precise than, and not so unduly generalized as, the third interpretation. The third, taken as such, involves nothing unique to the American situation. This third interpretation can avoid the two dangers we have emphasized only when it is related to peculiar socio-psychological problems which we experience as a nation. One may suggest as an instance of the latter the tragic paradox of the complacency that entices us as a powerful, "self-made" nation together with the despair we face in being unable to control our destiny in a hydrogen age. National peace of mind seems like our rightful inheritance and yet such peace of mind remains a desperate quest.

Additional factors may be at work beyond the considerations suggested by Herberg and other analysts. To mention one further possibility, it may be that part of the recent piety can be associated with the continually developing force of the practice of religious freedom, accelerated by the fact that our modern scientific culture, though challenging more traditional forms of piety, was nevertheless unable to expunge the religious propensities of men. In light of the great recent growth of piety, Herbert W. Schneider's assertion of only a half dozen years back seems extremely dated: "Religion is fighting for its life against strong cultural forces which treat it with indifference and disdain." [16]

Piety Anywhere

How is it, then, that the new religion has been able to spread so widely and so successfully? How is it, to return to an earlier example, that the entertainment world has come to assume an aura of piety? One could say that this particular trend is simply good business. This is a superficial reply. The socio-psychological atmosphere must be hospitable to developments such as these. In this regard, it must be kept in mind that agents of mass manipulation, for all their power over the living habits of the American people, are keenly sensitive to adverse public reaction.

We suggest, in sum, the following hypothesis as a possible orientation to the question of the roots of the surge of American piety: If the religion of the fathers, either as it was or, more probably, as it is imagined to have been, helps to provide essential social fulfillment along with psychological aid and comfort, and if, accordingly, it has become rather un-American to be unreligious,[17] then piety can and will break out just about anywhere—from the best-seller lists in the local bookstore to the prayer group in the nation's Capitol, and from the recently established department of religion in a thoroughly secular university to the juke box in the corner saloon. It follows that the important issues before us go beyond such a question of personal opinion as, "What do you think of Billy Graham?" The real issues involve the peculiar and ongoing socio-psychological processes of American life.

We must now engage in a more intensive consideration of the ways in which these processes may be revealed by actual religious trends.

Notes

1. Since 1926 the basis of reporting membership has been altered somewhat. For instance, a few bodies now report all baptized persons rather than just adults.

2. In 1954 the American Institute of Public Opinion maintained on the basis of a national survey that eight out of ten U.S. adults were church members, although the Institute pointed out that some people who claimed such membership may not actually have belonged to a particular congregation at that time.

3. The foregoing information is taken largely from the *Yearbook of the American Churches for 1958,* edited by Benson Y. Landis (New York: National Council of the Churches of Christ in the U.S.A., 1957), pp. 281 ff.

4. William Lee Miller, "Piety Along the Potomac," *The Reporter,* Aug. 17, 1954, p. 25.

5. Harry C. Meserve, "The New Piety," *The Atlantic,* June, 1955, p. 34.

6. Ronald Gregor Smith, "Man's Coming of Age," *The Listener* (published by the British Broadcasting Corporation), Apr. 4, 1957, p. 549. By permission of the author.

7. Reprinted by permission of the publishers from Herbert W.

Schneider, *Religion in 20th Century America* (Cambridge, Mass.: Harvard University Press, Copyright, 1952, by The President and Fellows of Harvard College), pp. 189-190.

8. Paul Hutchinson, "Have We a 'New' Religion?", *Life*, Apr. 11, 1955. By permission of Agnes M. Hutchinson, copyright owner.

9. On the basis of a national adult sample, the American Institute of Public Opinion reported on Dec. 17, 1954, the results of a poll on this question: "Figures show that there are more people going to church these days. How do you account for this increase in churchgoing?" The three most prevalent answers were "Fear, unrest, uncertainty of future," 30%; "Renewed faith in God as Supreme Being," 19%; and "Don't know," 22%. Though the respondents were not questioned on their own churchgoing habits, their views on the question asked could conceivably mirror somewhat the attitudes of the churchgoing population as a whole.

10. It is not our purpose to provide a complete listing of various attempts to account for the surge of piety in America.

11. From *Protestant-Catholic-Jew* by Will Herberg. Copyright © 1955 by Will Herberg, reprinted by permission of Doubleday & Company, Inc.

12. According to a survey conducted by *The Catholic Digest* in 1953, 95 per cent of the American people over 18 years of age declared themselves adherents of one or another of these three groups. A Gallup Poll made shortly thereafter (early in 1955) resulted in a figure of 96.9 per cent, although, as Herberg points out, this number considerably exceeds comparable membership lists maintained by the religious bodies. In February of 1958 the U.S. Census Bureau undertook a nation-wide sampling of 35,000 households, on the basis of which the Bureau submitted the following estimate: Among Americans 14 years old and over, there were within the current population as of March, 1957, 79 million Protestants, 30.7 million Roman Catholics, 3.9 million Jews, 1.5 million adherents of "some other religion," and 3.2 million people who claimed no religion.

13. The habit of lumping non-Catholics and non-Jews in the Protestant category illustrates the force of this trinitarianism. Eastern

Orthodox Christians in America often, and quite properly, protest against this practice.

14. See the review-article, "Sociology in Depth," by Alexander Miller and A. Roy Eckardt, *The Christian Scholar,* Dec., 1956, pp. 306-311.

We must not underestimate the survivalist urge that often persists among different ethnic groups in spite of assimilationist influence.

15. In Chapter Seven we consider this problem of conformist influences as a possible incitement to piety.

16. Schneider, *op. cit.,* p. 191.

17. This does not mean that the individual who fails to practice some form of piety is automatically subject to social ostracism. There are many people who in ways other than religious ones do not live up to the dominant social and moral standards of the culture and yet do not become outcasts.

In a city like New York the majority of the population has no religious affiliation. On the other hand, there remains a fairly widespread attitude among Americans that somehow our large cities do not really represent a fulfillment of the "American dream."

Chapter : T W O

Folk Religion: Its Ways and Works

So far we have seen that the recent "turn to religion" may be related positively to the unique story of our immigrant nation, with the accompanying critical pressures of twentieth-century American life contributing in some way to the trend as a whole. What characteristics of the surge of piety may we, accordingly, discern? In this chapter a general description will be followed by specific applications.

Folk Religion and Culture Religion

As an over-all descriptive term we suggest the phrase *folk religion*. This is an alternative to "culture religion," which has been employed by some interpreters. Granted our exposure to the writer's occupational disease of using different words to say the same thing, the term "culture religion" remains deficient at several points. Beyond the grammatical fault of permitting a noun to modify a noun,

42

the word "culture" (or "cultural" for that matter) cannot wholly escape association with highbrowism. To be sure, most of those who speak of "culture religion" are not thinking in this direction. They intend the phrase as a synonym for "social religion," in the sense of religion which is promoted by society and which itself promotes the common cause. Yet, the connotation we mention is there and it is misleading. The truth is that the recent American piety is not limited to highbrows in its appeal. So-called "cultured" people may, as a matter of fact, tend to look down their noses at overt forms of that piety for being at worst "common" and at best bourgeois.[1] But the real justification of the phrase "folk religion" is the fact that the "turn to religion" is very much a popular movement. As such, that development is asking for a term that fits it and helps to describe it.

The Meaning of Folk Religion

Folk religion is religion for the "folks." It is characterized by the fact that it holds both the people and religion in high esteem. It is a form of piety which seeks to promote individual and group "welfare." Conspicuous among its claims is that piety is a deliverer. Piety can resolve basic human problems of both a personal and a social nature, and this without very great difficulty. Religion is marked by its utility. It fosters individual security. It aids brotherhood. It contributes to social solidarity. In a word, religion is good because it is good for the people.

It is hardly necessary to add the corollary that from this point of view, the people are good for religion. The efforts, norms, and values of the people continually further the "cause of religion." Piety is eagerly promoted and conspicuously consumed in social life as a whole. Religion bears the stamp of social approval and the social interest bears the stamp of religious approval.

Focus on the Individual

When its emphasis falls upon the individual, folk religion in its American form proclaims a gospel of personal happiness, adjustment, and success. It is here that the work of Norman Vincent Peale comes inescapably to mind. Peale has received more attention than anyone else as representative of this point of view, although he is by no means a voice crying in the wilderness.[2]

In his most recent volume, *Stay Alive All Your Life,* Peale concedes that there is no such thing as easy living, that faith will not bring everything that a man wants, that to be worthy of immortality one's soul must be cleansed and brought in harmony with God, and that success is not to be equated with riches, fame, or power. Success means "the development of mature and constructive personality." Nor can we gain happiness by thinking only of ourselves. "It is a subtle and important fact that if we seek spiritual values only for ourselves they will turn dead in our hands; but when we receive and give, they replenish themselves."

Reservations such as these are few and far between in Peale's writings and preaching. They do not obscure the essence of his message. The dominant stress is upon personal self-fulfillment through the instrumentality of "faith." Religion is defined as "a scientific methodology for thinking your way through problems."

At the close of various chapters in *Stay Alive All Your Life* there is a list of steps for implementing the theme that Peale has just discussed. We have selected and combined a number of the items, in some cases using wording from the main text itself:

1. You can make your life what you want it to be through belief in God and in yourself.
2. Think success, believe in success, visualize success, and you set in motion the powerful force of the realizable wish.
3. Daily affirm enthusiasm. As you think it, talk it, and live it, you will have it.
4. Make peaceful thinking your permanent mental slant.
5. Overcome worry and live efficiently by substituting faith for fear.
6. Think big; believe big; pray big; act big.
7. Get outside of yourself. Do something every day for somebody. Bring joy to as many others as possible.
8. Get your personality organized and your thoughts tightened up. Effective thinking and action will result.
9. Practice hope. As hopefulness becomes a habit, you can achieve a permanently happy spirit.
10. Stay calm and serene. Do not fret or worry or allow yourself to become unnecessarily involved in situations fraught with emotion.
11. Empty out all resentment and hate.
12. The very moment you decide that nothing shall defeat you, from that instant *nothing can defeat you.*[3]

Focus on Society

When its emphasis falls upon social life, folk religion as a general human phenomenon affirms the interests of a particular group or nation or socio-economic policy. Religion is utilized for moral and spiritual support at the communal level.

With the rise of world communism as a menace to peace

and freedom, some Americans have turned to religion as a weapon in the struggle. This has seemed peculiarly justified by the fact that communism is ostensibly an atheistic movement which appears to threaten the values for which religion stands and even to flaunt the very purposes of God. Illustrative of the point of view here is International Christian Leadership, with headquarters in Washington, D.C. This organization sponsors breakfast, luncheon, and fireside groups, supports a speakers' bureau, and holds annual conferences which are addressed by eminent political leaders. It describes itself as "an informal association of concerned laymen banded together to find through Christ the better way of everyday living and to demonstrate and promote in home, community, nation and world a more effective Christian leadership." Up to the present our lives have not been all they should be. We can, nevertheless, develop a new life by seeking God's forgiveness, accepting Jesus Christ as Savior and Lord, and instituting such personal habits as private worship, Bible reading, and church attendance.

This does not sound, as such, like folk religion. The organization's monthly *Bulletin* often includes a reference to the importance of being led and judged by God. But the guiding spirit and incentive of International Christian Leadership is thoroughly utilitarian in character. Its program for "personal development" is candidly described as "a solution to today's troubles" through constructive action by men and women possessed of the "practical knowledge of how to help the other fellow." Though the word "International" appears in the name, the organization is frankly committed to the religious struggle against communism.

We believe that communism and other materialistic ideas find adherents only when Christian leadership falters or is absent. The power of Christ in the minds, hearts, and wills of leaders is the best hope that the free world will be strong enough and magnetic enough to command the loyalty of men everywhere.[4]

The stress upon human leaders as the best hope of the world is itself closely related to folk religion. But, more significantly, one of the spokesmen for this group has stated in the monthly *Bulletin* that

this is the crucial hour in a global warfare of living Christianity versus materialism and communism and all the anti-God and anti-Christ forces. You and I are called upon to help men and women off the fence to a clear-cut stand for Christ and His Kingdom. It is either-or. The time to decide and to act is now.[5]

The announced theme of one of the annual conferences held by this organization was "Living Christianity Versus Militant Materialism."

While International Christian Leadership includes the promotion of "freedom" as one of its several objectives, another group, Spiritual Mobilization, makes "freedom" its singular concern. With headquarters in Los Angeles, Spiritual Mobilization is somewhat more vocal than the other organization. Its publication, *Faith and Freedom,* has emphasized that the journal

is a voice of the libertarian—persistently recommending the religious philosophy of limited government inherent in the Declaration of Independence. The chief intent of the libertarian is not pedagogy, but the further discovery and application of the Creator's changeless principles in a changing world.

While speaking against the present-day Goliath, the totalitarian state, we work for no special interest. Freedom under God is in the interest of every man of faith, whether he is in a factory or on a farm, in an office or in the pulpit. If a government or a philosophy does not serve to safeguard his freedom—whether he is in a minority or a majority—then that government or philosophy is his enemy. A Communist, Socialist, Fascist or other authoritarian government is always such an enemy; and a democratic government espousing a paternalistic philosophy straightway becomes such an enemy.

As the journalists of Spiritual Mobilization, our editorial policy is based on a profound faith in God, the Author of liberty, and in Jesus Christ, who promoted persuasion in place of coercion as the means for accomplishing positive good.

Our credo is the long-standing credo of Spiritual Mobilization: Man, being created free as a child of God, has certain inalienable rights and responsibilities: the state must not be permitted to usurp them; it is the duty of the church to help protect them.

Spiritual Mobilization maintains that it works for no special interest. However, an obvious implication of the quoted statement is support for a "free enterprise" economy. Advocacy of such an economy is found in just about all the literature that Spiritual Mobilization has distributed.[6]

The Christian Freedom Foundation of New York City states its position more openly and in a way that equates the Christian faith itself with a particular economic and political philosophy. Its fortnightly paper, *Christian Economics,* indicates that "we stand for the free market—the economic system with the least amount of government and the greatest amount of Christianity."

The Theology of Folk Religion

The type of folk religion illustrated in the two sections above assumes that the decisive, guiding forces of the universe are positively impressed by certain people and groups of people and that these forces are prepared to come to terms with human wishes. God—if that is the correct term —helps those who help themselves or, more precisely, he helps those who practice piety.

To the extent that God has a place in folk religion, he is fundamentally helpmate, guide, and friend. If God should ever say or do anything against human interests— although folk religion would be hard put to conceive of the Divine acting this way—then so much the worse for God. Any religion inclining to the view that the divine purpose stands in some fundamental way in conflict with our purposes represents superstition or dogmatism or otherworldliness but not a faith that merits our attention or allegiance. A mature faith is one which recognizes that God's function is to conserve and implement human values.

Thus, essentially, God is on the side of people, or, more accurately, he is on the side of certain persons or a particular community or a particular nation. He is not necessarily happy with everyone but he is pleased with those who are his folk. We demonstrate that we are his folk by both moral and religious means. On the one hand, we seek to "lead good, clean lives" and, on the other hand, we say our prayers, read our Bibles, and attend church regularly. We are explicitly "religious" in ways that must be recognized as "good." [7]

Folk Religion and Billy Graham

Sometimes the Billy Graham evangelistic enterprise is cited as representative of folk religion as that phenomenon has been here identified. It is evident that within the

Graham movement there are tendencies opposite to those of folk piety. The stress in Graham's preaching upon human sin, the wrath and judgment of God, the corrosive evils of "secularism" and "materialism," and the necessity of subjecting ourselves to the divine will, no matter what the cost, is absent from most forms of folk religion. On the other hand, these very elements within the Graham message have not been immune to the pervasive influences of folk piety. Graham's type of evangelism is itself a peculiarly American phenomenon, coming down to us from the days of the frontier. It is worth noting that Graham castigates his audiences in a way which is noticeably blander than that of many of his predecessors, such as the famous Billy Sunday.

Further, Graham holds out many national hopes for the future. America is summoned to repent of its sins and to cast off its immoral ways, but the promise in this spiritual transformation will be the salvation of the land. America will come to take its rightful place in the counsels of the nations. The Lord will stay the hand of his wrath and deliver us into peace and true felicity. Thus, Graham has written that we are in need of a revolution if our nation is to be saved from destruction. This revolution will fight to overcome corruption in high places, immorality, licentiousness, and sensuality. The Christian church must lead the revolution.

We must somehow regain the spiritual fire and fervor of our forefathers. . . . If America turns fully to God, I submit that He can dispel the enemies of our country, both those within and those without, that God can blind their eyes and frustrate their plans, and give us victory and insure both peace and safety for unborn generations.[8]

Even if this theologizing were in some tacit way a preaching device to open men's hearts to the Christian message, we should have to charge Graham with hypocrisy if he did not mean what he has in fact said. This charge would be quite illicit. Like many contemporary representatives of a more unequivocal folk religion, Graham is widely admired for his sincerity and personal dedication. An alternative interpretation lies in recognizing that there are strong indications of the influence of folk piety upon the Graham version of Christianity.

It is impossible to come to terms with the Billy Graham phenomenon unless attention is paid to the way in which the evangelist as a personality embodies the American ideal of the fair-haired, handsome lad of boldness and integrity who is able to reach the top in his chosen calling. Part of Graham's popularity must be accounted for in this way, especially when it is remembered that for all his personal magnetism and gifts as a preacher, he refuses to go in for many of the theatrical devices of his revivalistic forebears and contemporaries. In the last analysis, Billy Graham is a man of the people, born of the folk, and consecrated to their eternal welfare. What more can the people ask of any man?

From the wide hearing Graham has gained it does not follow that the emphases in folk religion to which much of his message is opposed possess no effective power in American society. On the basis of the strength of commitment among Americans to their "way of life," there is ground for believing that if Graham were to go to extremes in condemning that way of life, his enterprise would be gravely threatened. Part of the recurring opposition to him may be, in fact, traceable to a repressed chauvinism. It is entirely possible that an acute state of national emergency would end Graham's influence over-night.

It may be mentioned in passing that even a proclama-tion of the wrath of God descending upon men can be softened at the hands of the folk. People tend to get used to the clergy telling them off, especially when the arraign-ment takes place within the relative anonymity of a group meeting or worship service. Preachers are rather "supposed to talk that way." The fact that the hearers "take it" with relative grace and sincere attention may, among its more socially approved results, help make them part of the crowd.

American Backgrounds

We have indicated that the common theme in folk re-ligion is piety in alliance with people, with what they interpret as their interests and ideals. Folk piety as such is maintained of, by, and for—not against—the people. The divergent voices of American folk religion are one in the conviction that there is in God—or at least in "spiritual resources"—something exceedingly useful to human pur-poses.

Once all this is said, we must face up to an analytical problem that was raised in a somewhat different connec-tion in Chapter One. In the discussion of the roots of the new piety, it was suggested that we must question interpre-tations which do not aid in a comprehension of the Amer-ican situation. A similar criticism could be made against the analysis thus far in this chapter. Folk religion is hardly limited to this nation. The Divine has been long employed for the furtherance of personal and social interests all over the world. It is true that our three "religions of democracy" have developed in ways unique to this country and, if Will Herberg is correct, it is also true that one or another of these faiths has come to furnish a significant socio-psychological home for innumerable individuals. There are, nevertheless, many differences of conviction and practice among the three faiths. Further, within American folk religion of the less institutional sort, there is considerable divergence of action and of opinion. Thus, for example, from one point of view religion is interpreted as a support of "free enterprise"; but from another point of view religious faith is held to justify the need for some degree of economic planning.[9]

We must, in consequence, try to be more precise. What is there about the American brand of folk piety that, generally speaking, gives evidence of association with its environment? What is the common background of our folk religion?

One possible answer lies in our general religio-political tradition. That tradition involves in large part an outgrowth and proliferation of at least two convictions, both of which are found in the New Testament: first, the governing authorities or the secular powers have been instituted of God; and, second, we must obey God, or a higher power, beyond our loyalties to men.[10] Since these convictions hardly permit any simple reconciliation, a society that, consciously or unconsciously, continues to seek to implement them will tend to arrive at a dynamic, or at least unstable, policy respecting the relation between religion and secular life.

The two convictions, when taken together, imply a number of mores, as these have been worked out in this country. No single item in the following list is unique to

American society. As we shall see, it is the combination of
the elements that is distinctive of our situation.

1. The temporal realm is essential and good. We have
a firm tradition of the importance of the socio-political
order and of social and political obligations. Men may
be blessed by life in nation and community. Democracy
is a basic value. The government and the state are fundamentally just institutions, in so far as they secure the consent of the governed, provide for basic human freedom
and justice, and in general serve the interests of the people.

2. The spiritual realm is essential and good. We have
a firm tradition of religious loyalty and freedom. No citizen can be denied the right to an independent, personal
relation with God. An obvious implication of this tradition is that religion can assume a great variety of forms.
The tradition has implied too that religion is entitled
to speak in judgment upon society, including the state.
If God is Lord over human life, it just may be that government will get in his way.

3. The temporal realm may be invaded by evil. We have
a firm tradition of limitations upon political authority.
Governments are tempted to exceed their powers, in
which eventuality it is incumbent upon men to obey a
higher order. The divine institution of the governing authorities provides no guarantee that they will not seek to
become tyrannical.

4. The spiritual realm may be invaded by evil. We have
a firm tradition of suspicion of religious authority. Religion may fall into corruption, especially if a "religious
establishment" were ever to be instituted. Here is much
of the ground of the principle of separation of church and
state. If the secular powers are divinely instituted, it just
may be that religion will get in God's way. Loyalty to

religion is not to hinder brotherhood or make for social conflict. The spiritual realm is kept from becoming bad through emphasis upon common "spiritual values."

This set of mores has evolved into a combination quite peculiar to the American situation. When we surrendered the Puritan theocratic ideal of the holy commonwealth we made possible a free society. In modern America the forces of religion stop short of any complete hegemony over, or condemnation of, the state. They are not supposed to harbor even for a moment unwholesome thoughts of clerical dominion over the temporal realm. Indeed, if religion makes critical judgments of society, this is, ideally, only because society's ultimate interests are at stake. Religion's support of democracy is associated with the Judeo-Christian conviction of the sacredness of human personality and also, to a lesser extent, with the conviction that men stand under the necessity of social constraint.

As Reinhold Niebuhr's oft-quoted aphorism states it, "Man's capacity for justice makes democracy possible; but man's inclination to injustice makes democracy necessary." With our dauntless optimism, we have come in our ideology to stress the former element much more than the latter. Though we have never wholly lost the Puritan consciousness of sin, we have tended to reduce sin to a moral problem that can be taken care of through proper nurture in American spiritual values. The prevalent ideal is that religion, like government, should serve the commonweal, although not at the expense of religious freedom. In effect, the reason religious freedom is praiseworthy is that it too is, in the last resort, good for the people. As a matter of fact, religious freedom itself is not without restriction. Not only must that freedom provide the soil for building the character of the citizenry, but also, as a matter of practice,

religious freedom has come primarily to mean freedom for
the three "religions of democracy." We do not censure
additional religious groups politically or legally but we
more or less assume—not of necessity in a calculating way—
the priority of Christianity together with (more recently)
Judaism.

Spiritual domination of temporal affairs would mean
clericalism. We acknowledge and rationalize our fears here
through such slogans as "business is business." Religion
must not trespass unduly into areas of life that are not
its proper concern. On the other hand, temporal domination of spiritual affairs would mean dictatorship. We try
to forestall that evil eventuality through such an ideological principle as "in this country a man can believe
as he pleases" and, when occasion demands, by the
churches actually standing up to political menaces to
their integrity. Separation of church and state helps keep
theocracy away; religious freedom militates against secular and political tyranny.

In ways such as these opportunity is provided for our
brand of folk religion to grow. Religion is good but,
should it turn its back on the people, it becomes evil.
Needless to say, supplementary historical influences have
also operated, such as our pioneering experience with its
promotion of humanistic values and interests and reliance
upon human resourcefulness.

Several analytical reservations are in order here. It is
not claimed that the religio-political situation just
sketched is the ultimate or the direct cause of contemporary American folk religion. Nor is it alleged that our
triple melting-pot arrangement accounts in an exhaustive
or primary way for the various forms of folk piety. Further, the question of why men exalt themselves and their

collectivities to a decisive position in their total religious life is not here considered. The most we can say is that the over-all American religio-political arrangement provides fundamental opportunity for the several species of folk religion to assert themselves. The point is that something must be at work to serve to domesticate Christianity and Judaism to the demands of folk religion.

The Domestication of Faith

For the American citizen, the Protestant, Catholic, and Jewish faiths tend to furnish a psychosocial resting place. This is in contrast to the sort of faith which allegedly enshrines the final truth of God, a being to whom men ought to commit themselves quite independently of specific "good" consequences that may follow. The background for the American brand of folk religion—let us say its necessary, although not sufficient, condition—is our general religio-political arrangement, which provides religion with freedom and importance but always within the restrictions noted above. When the trinitarian character of American institutional religion is associated with this religio-political arrangement, the over-all picture is one of faith under arrest and piety under restraint. Protestantism, Catholicism, and Judaism combine with less institutional aspects of American folk piety to form a body of religion distinguished and limited by elements of utilitarianism, this-worldly activism, and moral concern, surrounded by an atmosphere of religious pluralism, tolerance, and optimism. The Protestant teaching that salvation is a free gift of divine grace quite apart from all human effort, the Catholic insistence that the Church of Rome is the one true church, and the Jewish persuasion

that the Jews are the peculiarly chosen people of the Lord
have alike either been soft-pedaled or essentially reformu-
lated to accord with the responsibilities of the faithful as
citizens of this democracy.

F. Ernest Johnson speaks of the paradox that derives
from American cultural pluralism. In our pluralistic culture the unhampered, spontaneous expression of individuality is stressed. But there also obtains the necessity of
co-operation in implementing the values that support
American society as a collective entity.[11] Meanwhile, the
many less institutional aspects of the new piety can, under
the sanctions of religious liberty, develop a variegated
mixture, yet always channeled by the limiting, ostensibly
benevolent framework of "the American way of life." In
sum, the Christian and Jewish faiths have been considerably domesticated to American ideals and practice, and so
has folk religion in general.

We have a few times used the expression "the American way of life." Such elements in American religion as
utilitarianism, activism, morality, pluralism, and tolerance are, of course, part and parcel of that "way of life,"
even though, to be sure, no one of these ideals had its
ultimate origin in American culture. If we are to account
for the fact that the conflicting differences within the
three major faiths as well as within less institutional aspects of folk religion have involved a minimum of social
conflict, we must turn to the peculiar pattern that the
set of ideals above has come to assume in American life.
Or, more positively, we must look to the overarching faith
that unites Americans beyond their several religious
allegiances.

Will Herberg's study again offers relevant insight. Herberg takes as his point of departure here a suggestion of

Robin M. Williams, Jr., that a society tends to be intolerant of opposition to its ultimate values. Since individual Americans do not incline to display very great intolerance toward those two of the three religions of democracy of which they are not themselves members, it would seem that no one part of the trinity of American popular piety finds its holiness in its own exclusive claims but finds it instead in its contribution to some other, more holy end. What is this other end? Or, in alternate phrasing, what is it of which Americans are intolerant? The answer is that they are intolerant of what stands in opposition to "the American way of life."

The American Way of Life is, at bottom, a spiritual structure, a structure of ideas and ideals, of aspirations and values, of beliefs and standards; it synthesizes all that commends itself to the American as the right, the good, and the true in actual life. . . . When in the *Ladies' Home Journal* poll [of 1948] Americans were asked "to look within themselves and state honestly whether [they] thought [they] really obeyed the law of love [of neighbor] under certain special conditions, 90 per cent said yes and 5 per cent no when the one to be "loved" was a person belonging to a different religion; 80 per cent said yes and 12 per cent no when it was the case of a member of a different race; 78 per cent said yes and 10 per cent no when it concerned a business competitor—but only 27 per cent said yes and 57 per cent no in the case of "a member of a political party that you think is dangerous," while 25 per cent said yes and 63 per cent said no when it concerned an enemy of the nation. . . . [These figures reflect] how seriously Americans take transgressions against the law of love in various cases. Americans feel they *ought* to love their fellow men despite differences of race or creed or business interest; that is what the American Way of Life emphatically prescribes. But the American Way of Life almost explicitly sanctions hating a member of a "dangerous" political party (the Communist party is obviously meant here) or an enemy of one's country, and therefore an overwhelming majority avow their hate. In both situations, while the Jewish-Christian law of love is formally acknowledged, the truly operative factor is the value system embodied in the American Way of Life. Where the American Way of Life approves of love of one's fellow man, most Americans confidently assert that they practice such love; where the American Way of Life disapproves, the great mass of Americans do not hesitate to confess that they do not practice it, and apparently feel very little guilt for their failure. No better pragmatic test as to what the operative religion of the American people actually is could be desired.[12]

Billy Graham has indicated that he is much impressed by the current "revival" of religion. On the occasion of an address to a group of students at the Union Theological Seminary in New York City, Graham

read off a list of [signs of the revival] and among them was the back-to-God movement sponsored by the American Legion. It was interesting that when he came to this on his list, his whole audience laughed. He did not have the slightest idea as to why they laughed. He was obviously puzzled and said: "You must have had this in a class." Also, he emphasized at another point the work of Dr. Peale with obvious approval. He was present at the prayer breakfast in Washington attended by the President and most of the Cabinet and he was uncritically impressed by the whole affair.[13]

In the light of Graham's avowed and strong commitment to an evangelical and fundamentalist version of Christian faith,[14] these expressions of approval are very interesting. The "signs" Graham mentioned hardly accord with the central emphasis in his own Christian position. It may be, as John C. Bennett observes, that Graham simply fails to be sufficiently discriminating in his religious judgments. But it may be too that Graham stands here under the influence of "the American way of life." [15] It is difficult to find two religious leaders with messages of more diametrically opposed themes than Billy Graham and Norman Vincent Peale. Yet, on his part, Peale, for example, participated in the 1957 Graham "crusade" in New York City. What is it that unites these two men? As a minimum, we must refer to their common conviction that religion is a very good thing. This cardinal assumption of American folk religion blends extremely well with the spirituality of "the American way of life."

Folk Religion Through the Back Door

An ironic eventuality in any treatment of folk religion is the unacknowledged conditioning of the assessor at the hands of folk religion itself. Ever since Puritan days the American people, in passing judgment on overt forms of religion, have come under the sway of certain, usually unannounced presuppositions. Typical of these assumptions are, on the one hand, the essentially personal, inner quality of the religious life and, on the other hand, the central place in religion of demands for personal and social righteousness. He who finds fault with various institutional and social expressions of the new piety, whatever his own conscious purposes, shows his consistency with a basic element in the American outlook. As Herbert W. Schneider has put it, the "notion that religion is religiosity, and that a cultus is either idolatry or foolishness, is shared by some of the most pious and the most impious Americans." [16] Perhaps the different forms of religion are mere empty formalism, and the protestations of the religious mere Pharisaism. Here is illustrated a prophetic influence that is highly critical of folk religion. But note the paradox. The prophetic heritage of the American people has, in turn, been colored by their own cultural point of view.

To put worship into the context of the "amenities and courtesies" of polite society is offensive to the "shirtsleeve" informality and equalitarianism of American life and smacks of hypocrisy. A ceremonial sacrifice is not a real sacrifice and a ritualistic penance may not express real contrition.[17]

Or, in the language of the foregoing description of folk religion, the cultus itself may prove not to be really good for the people. It then becomes suspect.

All this provides part of the basis for the extremely mixed reactions that have emerged respecting the work of Billy Graham. From one point of view, Graham's campaigns, like those of many earlier evangelists, break through with refreshing vitality the crust of religious formalism. The use of "Billy" as a form of address is itself a perfect symbol of one side of our way of life, standing in delightful contrast to such proper appellations as "His Eminence" and "The Most Reverend." [18] The evangelical proclamation of "the faith of our fathers" can be a compelling social summons—particularly when there is such gross and happy ignorance of the anything but humanistic nature of much of the old religion. The summons also serves to bring to the surface blessed memories of creative men through whose patient labor the old faith is somehow living still. Is it not fitting that we today should rediscover the "old-time religion"? To quote again from Herbert W. Schneider, the gospel of olden times "has acquired the value of an antique. . . . Sentimentalism is a genuine trait in the American people, and their worship will naturally reflect this trait." [19] This total attitude is given a decisive personal touch by means of the revivalist call to strengthen the inner spiritual life through Bible study and prayer. Finally, in denouncing the sins of contemporary American life, Billy Graham appeals strongly to our moral, and perhaps rather moralistic, sense.

From a contrasting point of view, the Graham campaigns furnish ammunition for those who stand ever ready to point the accusing finger at the respectable hypocrites who place their piety on exhibition in such public temples as Madison Square Garden, New York. Churchmen may applaud Graham's stress—in contrast to the anti-institutionalism of many revivalists of the old school—upon cooperation with the churches of the community and his acknowledgment of the institutional Christian church as an instrument of God and indeed the Body of Christ. Yet, iconoclasts can lament with equal vigor Graham's refusal to break completely with the churches, those skeletons of a dead institutionalism. Accompanying voices are raised against the evangelist's failure to apply in tangible ways the moral emphases of his preaching to such urgent social issues as racial segregation. Graham has also been criticized—most notably by Reinhold Niebuhr—for his oversimplified solutions to social and moral problems. Such criticism presupposes the need for a constructive orientation to these problems, else the charge would be pointless. However, with this particular criticism we are in a crucial way carried beyond the area of mixed reactions to Graham from within a peculiarly American cultural perspective. Americans as a whole can hardly be accused of any fear of simplicity.[20]

The Attractions of Folk Religion

How influential is the American version of folk piety? How representative is it of the religious standards, ideals, and practices that derive from the inner character of Americans as a people? Herbert W. Schneider believes that the point of view of the vast majority of the American people is to "take religion for granted as a ready help in time of trouble," rather than as something requiring a daily regimen. At the point of worship, need rather than duty prevails.[21] Schneider's generalization is rather too cynical. To employ religion as a helper and to turn honestly to God for help are not on quite the same level. Further, it is important to remember that many contemporary varieties of folk religion are relatively new to the total religious scene. These varieties may come, of course, to exert continuing social influence, even after they themselves run their course.

On the other side, to the extent that folk religion as identified in this chapter is hardly the sort of thing that Americans can be counted on to resist, Schneider is right. Forms of religion that reputedly foster immediate human welfare and satisfy immediate human wishes will tend to call out a certain approving response among men. Many of our people will probably count the recent forms of piety a blessing, rather than qualifying their judgments or reacting in terms of disapproval. Such approving response is itself a revelation of folk religion. Is not religion, after all, a good thing? [22]

Notes

1. American intellectuals, although by and large middle class in their pocketbooks, are nevertheless tempted to highbrowism in their responses to the passing scene. Though a number in this group have been influenced somewhat by the contemporary revival of interest in theology, they remain quite skeptical and even censorious of less intellectualistic expressions of religion. Consider, for example, their critical reactions to the revivalism of Billy Graham and the faith healing of Oral Roberts.

2. Norman Vincent Peale's point of view is evaluated in Chapter Four.

3. Adapted from *Stay Alive All Your Life* by Dr. Norman Vincent Peale, © 1957 by Prentice-Hall, Inc., published by Prentice-Hall, Inc., Englewood Cliffs, N.J. Used by permission.

4. From a leaflet, "Objectives and Methods, International Christian Leadership."

5. Abraham Vereide in the *Bulletin of International Christian Leadership*, Nov., 1954.

6. Until recently the statement reproduced above has appeared as part of the masthead of *Faith and Freedom*. In most recent issues the following statement has been substituted: "We believe the following ideas need to permeate life. And we believe Spiritual Mobilization can provide an emphasis now lacking; We believe that each man is potentially of supreme worth and should work to achieve spiritual and creative wholeness; We believe that when men force their wills upon others, even for 'their own good,' it frustrates man's basic need. We see this today primarily in uncontrolled political intervention and the excesses of the labor union movement; We believe that spiritual and moral leaders must resist—not promote—the abuses of power which destroy man's integrity of spirit."

   The current literature circulated by Spiritual Mobilization indicates that socio-economic libertarianism remains as the avowed point of view of the organization. There is no evidence that the group has in any way retracted the position affirmed in the earlier statement.

7. The group-centered variety of folk religion, as outlined under the last two headings, is appraised critically in Chapter Six.

8. Billy Graham, "What's Wrong with American Morals," *The American Weekly*, May 12, 1957.

9. For an illustration of the latter position, in rather extreme but transparent form, see the writings of John Macmurray, for whom Socialism is *the* economic embodiment of Christianity. Macmurray is an Englishman, but his writings have had some influence on American religious intellectuals.

10. Compare Romans 13:1 and Acts 5:29.

11. F. Ernest Johnson, ed., *Patterns of Faith in America Today* (New York: Harper & Brothers, 1957), Introduction, p. 2.

12. From *Protestant-Catholic-Jew* by Will Herberg. Copyright 1955 by Will Herberg. Reprinted by permission of Doubleday & Company, Inc., New York. Pp. 87-90.

13. John C. Bennett, "Billy Graham at Union," *Union Seminary Quarterly Review*, May, 1954, pp. 10-11.

14. See Billy Graham's book, *Peace with God* (Garden City, N. Y.: Doubleday & Company, Inc., 1953). "Christianity finds all its doctrines stated in the Bible, and the true Christian denies no part, nor attempts to add anything to the Word of God. While the Constitution of the United States may be amended from time to time no amendment is ever necessary for the Bible. We truly believe that the men who wrote the Bible were guided by the Holy Spirit, both in the thoughts they expressed and in their choice of words." (P. 27.) Copyright 1953 by Billy Graham, reprinted by permission of Doubleday & Company, Inc.

15. Bennett stresses, however, that Graham's grasp of biblical Christian faith helps to counterbalance his involvement in the new American piety. "He told us that the message to America should be primarily one of judgment, and that the message to Britain should be primarily one of love. That is too simple but it is a rough way of stating a truth and would not be readily appre-

ciated at a Washington prayer breakfast." (Bennett, *op. cit.*, p. 12.)

16. Herbert W. Schneider, *Religion in 20th Century America* (Cambridge, Mass.: Harvard University Press, 1952), p. 147.

17. *Ibid.*

18. Such usage also has the tantalizing effect of making people who refer to "Billy" sound sympathetic when such is not their intent. The author recalls one written discussion of Graham in which the analyst simply refused to employ the nickname and referred always to the Reverend William Graham.

19. Schneider, *op. cit.*, p. 148.

20. The Billy Graham version of piety is given systematic evaluation in Chapter Five.

21. Schneider, *op. cit.*, pp. 167, 145.

22. It is a moot point whether an appraisal of folk religion can be made in ways free from the influence of folk religion itself. We are aware that this chapter has opened up the very perplexing question of whether it is possible to achieve a transcendent perspective for making religious judgments upon religion. This difficulty receives explicit attention in Chapter Eight.

Chapter : THREE

An Irreverent Intrusion: Ironic Hazards
in the New Religion

In this and succeeding chapters a perspective is sought for evaluating the religious trends that are before us.

The practice of tailoring religion to fit personal, group, and national interest is nothing new under the sun. It extends deep into the history of the race and, on a much reduced scale of time and intensity, well back into the history of this country. The fact that folk religion is perennial in human affairs does not reduce the necessity for critical understanding and judgment in the here and now. The moral life means trying to cope with the same old problems amidst new circumstances.

On reflection many will conclude that there is both good and bad in folk religion. Its weaknesses and temptations must be opposed, but, even as men seek to correct its half-truths, they ought to allow for whatever it offers that is worth while. Such, indeed, is the double standpoint from which the present study is written—although our particular understanding of "worth while" always entails a consciously Christian point of view.

The Elusiveness of Motivation

The most baffling problem for a study such as this is the serious and permanent limitation upon a concrete measurement and appraisal of the quality of those inner concerns that lead people to religious behavior. An individual has a hard enough time comprehending his own motives; how much more difficult it is for an external observer to judge them. This predicament provides one analytical comfort: Any blanket condemnation of the American turn to piety on grounds of dubious motivation is morally out of order. Where doubt is present its benefit must be freely given.

No question is raised here concerning the sincerity of the proponents of the new religion. Were insincerity or lack of integrity discernible, the recent piety would offer much less legitimate ground of appeal than it possesses and it would be much easier to appraise. (Almost needless to say, the individual's grasp of the meaning and import of his church's or religious group's preaching and teaching may bear little resemblance to reactions on the part of an objective onlooker.) The task of assessing the new piety must be consciously restricted to accord with the elusiveness of motivation.

It is not unwarranted, however, to pay attention to overt, tangible aspects of the "turn to religion" and to inquire concerning their fruits. The evaluative thesis of this study as a whole is that there are certain ironic strains in the surge of piety in America.

The Meaning of Irony

We are adopting Reinhold Niebuhr's usage of irony in *The Irony of American History*. Niebuhr employs the concept in a way that distinguishes irony from both pathos and tragedy.

Irony consists of apparently fortuitous incongruities in life which are discovered, upon closer examination, to be not merely fortuitous. Incongruity as such is merely comic. It elicits laughter. This element of comedy is never completely eliminated from irony. But irony is something more than comedy. A comic situation is proved to be an ironic one if a hidden relation is discovered in the incongruity. If virtue becomes vice through some hidden defect in the virtue; if strength becomes weakness because of the vanity to which strength may prompt the mighty man or nation; if security is transmuted into insecurity because too much reliance is placed upon it; if wisdom becomes folly because it does not know its own limits—in all such cases the situation is ironic. The ironic situation is distinguished from a pathetic one by the fact that the person involved in it bears some responsibility for it. It is differentiated from tragedy by the fact that the responsibility is related to an unconscious weakness rather than to a conscious resolution. While a pathetic or a tragic situation is not dissolved when a person becomes conscious of his involvement in it, an ironic situation must dissolve, if men or nations are made aware of their complicity in it. Such awareness involves some realization of the hidden vanity or pretension by which comedy is turned into irony. This realization either must lead to an abatement of the pretension, which means contrition; or it leads to a desperate accentuation of the vanities to the point where irony turns into pure evil.[1]

The fundamental question for our inquiry is whether there is reasonable hope that different forms of the new piety will bring about the results their proponents claim—claims for which these people have assumed personal responsibility. To the extent that the answer must be in the negative, we have an ironic situation. It will not be maintained that the recent forms of piety must prove to be complete failures—this is not our point of view—but only that there are conspicuously ironic elements within these religious forms. Much of the motivation in restricting ourselves to the theme of irony is the avoidance of an unduly condemnatory and holier-than-thou attitude. Our hope is to contribute a little to the search for critical understanding. As Niebuhr puts it, in irony weakness is unconscious. In the great majority of cases, adherents of the new piety "mean well" in the praiseworthy sense of that term.

Intellectuals and the Simple Life

A fundamental component of irony is simplification, spilling over with ease into oversimplification. Before taking up specific manifestations of irony within the "turn to religion," we do well at least to *raise* the question of whether our very introduction of the issue of irony is merely symptomatic of the well-known "egghead" phobia of simplification. (That reference is made to this possibility may thus echo an ironic strain within the present analysis.)

Is life really as complicated as the professors tend to make it? Alfred North Whitehead, a man far more brilliant than most of us, used to point out that in order to live, men are forced to simplify. Someone has remarked that all the philosophers in the world laid end to end seldom reach a conclusion. This diagnosis is sometimes applied to the professorial class as a whole. A popular stereotype has the "egghead" committed to an almost interminable analysis of problems, in a way that avoids responsible, practical action.

Whether or not this charge has some validity, the question of the complexities in human life cannot be decided on the basis of who talks the longest and who talks the least. The presence or absence of complexity is a matter not for sheer intellectuality but for living experience to adjudicate. Whitehead insisted too that while men are forced to seek simplicity, they must also distrust it.

Simplification is a uniting bond amidst diverse forms of folk religion. A great deal of our resurgent piety comes down to religion by formula. The general formula for problem solving reads, "If we believe or act in terms of A, then B—the desired effect—will follow." Apostles of the new religion put meat on the formula's bones in varied ways. According to the devotee of peace of mind piety, "If I galvanize my inner resources, I can conquer my frustrations and make myself a success." For the contemporary revivalist, "If we repent and get converted, our perplexities will be resolved." From the point of view of the religious nationalist, "If America will turn to God, the destructive and godless forces that threaten to destroy her will be confounded." For the economic libertarian, "If the system of 'free enterprise' is restored, men will enter upon their just inheritance of a truly free and abundant life."

Is religion by formula necessarily valid—even on its own terms? Let us turn to an appraisal of the specific religious trends we have outlined.

Note

1. Reinhold Niebuhr, *The Irony of American History* (New York: Charles Scribner's Sons, 1952), p. viii. Used by permission.

Chapter : FOUR

Ironic Strains in "The Cult of Reassurance"

Owing largely to their earthly opportunities and success as a people, Americans have been predominantly, to use William James' language, "healthy-minded" rather than "sick-souled." It is not simply the tragic world experiences of this century that have brought about a more sick-souled outlook. The very knowledge of sick-souled predispositions forced upon people ever since Sigmund Freud may have itself compounded the effective force of these predispositions.

The New Anxiety

Anxiety has become somewhat of a fashion. To be reminded again and again how anxious they probably are deep down underneath is enough to make many men conclude that they must really be quite anxious after all. Sophisticated doubts are raised concerning the possibility of being normal and even the normality of being normal. We live in an acutely psychological age. Ironically enough, men just may talk themselves into personality problems which simply did not occur with such compulsion to their less self-conscious forefathers.

Psychology, much more than religion, has brought about this intense state of self-awareness and introspection. Traditionally, it is primarily through religion that men are reminded of their moral and spiritual illnesses. But religion in this country has been remarkably conditioned by an idealistic and optimistic view of life and, hence, has in general been somewhat deficient in fulfilling the function just mentioned. In the meantime, however, psychologists have been increasingly lifting into our consciousness the force of our rationalizations, guilt, and anxiety. Partly as an outgrowth of this trend, religion has begun to ally itself more and more with psychology in the task of treating the anxieties—whether objectively caused or self-induced may not make a decisive practical difference —which earlier forms of religion had either not known or had unreflectively lumped under the all-devouring heading of sin. To the new task many clergymen have come to devote their energies.

Men are hardly to be blamed for seeking *some kind* of fundamental assurance in this world. It is really inevitable that they do so, simply because they are beings possessed of self-consciousness, who know by both experience and anticipation the menace of suffering, death, and meaninglessness. If only for the sake of the discussion, but preferably out of charity too toward ourselves and others, let us take seriously the assumption of folk piety that religion ought to help people. Pleas in behalf of individual well-being serve as their own justification. But is any particular instance of this variation on the theme of folk religion necessarily humane? In specific cases it may be incumbent upon us to meet representations of this point of view on their own ground. If anyone denies the importance of assurance and of religion's role (among its other possible functions) in furnishing assurance and providing power for meeting life's problems, he may be accused, not unjustifiably, of inhumaneness. Here, then, is the problem: How genuine are the particular assurances men come to accept?

The High Priest of the Cult

The preceding question may be addressed to Norman Vincent Peale as the most popular contemporary exponent of a certain form of psychologically oriented piety. Paul Hutchinson has referred to Peale as the high priest of the cult of reassurance.

From all evidences, Peale is an extremely unselfish, other-centered, and dedicated man. In the presence of his colossal efforts to help people, few can escape the force of Jesus' question, "What more are you doing than others?" We must grant too a measure of realism in Peale's approach. It is seldom that men act affirmatively apart from a certain calculation of self-interest. It is seldom too that they act from complete purity of motive. Peale appears to understand well that one way men are moved to action is through their own personal concerns. In this, Peale is wiser than the idealist who expects that mere referral to the good must spark the flame of goodness within.

Nevertheless, Peale's approach provides its own ironic limitations. Many of these flow from Peale's own version of idealism respecting human nature, as also from his general psychological presuppositions. No matter how sick-souled people may be in these times—and no one plays upon the theme of their anxiousness more than Peale—restoration to healthy-mindedness becomes on his view an exceedingly simple operation.

Attention is called to an evaluation of Peale's work by a leading student in the psychology of religion and pastoral counseling, Wayne E. Oates.[1] Oates' commentary is a relatively objective and balanced one, fairly typical of the sort of appraisal some Christian scholars versed in psychology are making of the work of Peale and of spokesmen for closely related points of view. Oates is not hostile. He in no way wishes to detract from "the real contribution which such approaches as those of Dr. Peale apparently make to the lives of some people."

Oates emphasizes the importance of giving due weight to the milieu in which Norman Vincent Peale carries on his work. As pastor of a church in New York City, Peale operates within

a highly transient culture of uprooted people. Among these people, great numbers are "cakes half-turned"—raw on one side with the new ideas of half-baked, sophisticated philosophies current in the Towers of Babel of New York City; burned to a crisp on the other side with the competitive secularism of American business. Into the emptiness, meaninglessness, and confusion created by these two forces, Norman Vincent Peale preaches, teaches, and writes. . . .

In addition, Oates singles out three reasons for the appeal in an approach like Peale's.

1. He has recaptured many of the tattered remnants of the badly disorganized religious traditions of the American people. These remnants live on in the stories which he tells. The

proverbs, epigrams, and stories he tells have different versions in the childhood memories of many Americans. The "broken chords" of religious devotion "vibrate once more" in many of these stories.

2. Dr. Peale has the courage to say the obvious among a generation of preachers who are struggling to say something profound, different, and unusual. He has a sort of cafeteria— or automat—religion in which what he has to offer is often so obvious that the person has only to reach out and get it, *for whatever it is worth to him if it appeals to his fancy.*

3. Dr. Peale has reaffirmed two basic ideas that men and women are desperately eager to believe: (a) the reality of hope, i.e., that in the midst of despair there is such a thing as hope *for them as individuals;* (b) the ability and responsibility of each man and woman to do something tangible about his own situation. . . . [Peale's] sermons become the paregoric of the tense, unloved, lonely, fearful, purposeless, fretful masses who buy, read, and wear out his books.

On the other side, Oates makes clear that a number of serious psychological errors appear in Peale's teaching and method. Several of these are relevant to our thesis of ironic strains in the new piety. Though Peale attempts to use resources from modern psychology, much in his theory and method is extremely dubious, having been subjected to severe criticism by many psychologists.[2] Peale subscribes to a conditioned-reflex theory of personality whereby, at the individual's own conscious desire, the self can supposedly be conditioned, reconditioned, and reconditioned again. He assumes that the prevailing drive in human beings is to become exactly what they wish and imagine themselves to be. This view may have some credence with respect to completely healthy personalities (who, of course, hardly need Peale's help), but what about the many ordinary people and the numbers of really disturbed people who are exposed to the Peale message? Peale's strictures against "negative thoughts" do not meet the issue of repression, that tendency, possessed in some measure by all of us, to force below consciousness a conscious drive or wish without actually coming to terms with it. The blotting out of "negative thoughts" not only raises the moral question of honesty with one's self but may actually aggravate one's worries. As Oates puts it,

to have unhappy thoughts is certainly an unhappy thing. A doubly unhappy thing is to have unhappy thoughts *over having unhappy thoughts!* . . . these prescriptions easily push a really depressed person into a deeper despair when the easy answers do not work.

Peale employs freely the device of reassurance. Though reassurance can be an important preliminary aid in healing, its continual use tends to numb the individual to his real needs and to prevent him from achieving a real understanding of himself and his problems. The role of *insight,* which so many psychologists see as all-important, is almost entirely missing from Peale's writings. Oates believes that addiction to reassurance helps greatly to explain Peale's popularity among many neurotics.

Freedom, Fate, and a Final Formula

The call to men to marshal their God-given resources for "effective living" may be justified and even demanded in particular situations—as where sloth and irresponsibility have gained control. Not only is it true that, in Erich Fromm's words, man "cannot accept himself as dice thrown out of the cup," but, in addition, one of the great dangers in the non-Communist world today is that of defeatism. Should not any call to action be balanced, nevertheless, by the forcefully expressed recognition that the human spirit is subject to fateful influences beyond its ability to master? [3] Is it necessarily the case that the average individual can lift himself by his own bootstraps or even "with the help of God" to wherever he wants to go? In one of his sermons Peale says,

You have to get in tune with God and tell yourself at the start of each day, "Another great day has begun." . . . You can be what you have pictured, and accomplish what you want your life to be. . . . The formula for good days ahead is to pray hard, work hard, believe hard—and picture hard.[4]

Will the summons to make something of oneself by such means, religious or otherwise, necessarily provide real inspiration? Or will it not simply compound the fears that "normal" people have, arising from day-to-day moral and spiritual failings? [5]

Peale emphasizes that religious counsel must take seriously psychological teaching. It is ironic that at his hands a science capable of doing much to help people is simplified and distorted in ways that may bring harm in the long run. In so far as there is serious error in Peale's approach, his great desire to help people must remain unfulfilled. Thus may "virtue become vice through a hidden defect in the virtue."

Moreover, there are grave questions concerning the professional ethics of writing books, articles, and columns which offer generalized advice that cannot possibly take into account the specific case history and situation of the individual. This is one of the weightiest reasons that disturbed people should avoid such sources and seek out instead a counselor who can work with them on a face-to-

face basis. Unfortunately—or perhaps fortunately—every
individual's psychological condition is a unique affair that
has little parallel to such generalized treatment as is possible, for example, in a purely physical problem like pro-
tection against polio. Indeed, even in the "physical" area
there is no substitute for individual attention. Refuge in
the written word as a psychological nostrum itself contains
an ironic twist. People are most often in need of resources
through which they may be accepted as individual human
beings. All they succeed in getting through the written
word is treatment in the mass.

Nor are the generalizations within such impersonal
treatment necessarily veracious. It would be sobering to
learn how American Negroes will react to this story from
Stay Alive All Your Life:

A Negro boy said to me glumly, "I can never amount to
much in this country."

"Why not?" I asked.

"You ought to know," he answered.

"You are healthy, aren't you?" I asked. "And smart?"

He grinned and agreed.

"You have a good mother? A good father?"

He nodded.

"Let me feel your muscle."

He rolled up his sleeves and grinned again when I con-
gratulated him on his well-developed muscles.

"And you have a wonderful smile." I added this item to his
assets.

"But I am colored," he objected.

"So is Ralph Bunche, who used to be a janitor," I reminded
him. "So is Jackie Robinson. So is the President of the Borough
of Manhattan, Hulan Jack." And I went on to mention others.
"Your thinking is twenty-five years behind the times, son. Then

it was more difficult for Negro men and women, but some of them did mighty well, all the same." [6]

Peale then told the boy of a man at a country fair who said, speaking of balloons, "It isn't the color that determines how high they go, but the stuff inside them that counts."

I added for my young friend, "If you will get self-doubt out of your mind, and rid yourself of the inferiority complex you are nursing, and believe that God will help you, and then if you give everything you have to whatever you do, you will get along all right." [7]

Perhaps all this may inspire a few Negroes. But for most of them, we should imagine, it merely reflects an ideology, wearisome in its repetition, purveyed by someone with the fortune to be possessed of a white skin—not to mention the raw materials and the type of environment conducive to the development of a dominant personality. The simple truth is that Norman Vincent Peale committed a basic error in fact and thereby misled the Negro lad. He did not *mean* to do this. But he does bear moral responsibility for what he said and for reproducing the advice in his book; hence, irony is present. The boy's thinking was *not* twenty-five years behind the times. Instances of good fortune among Negroes point up tellingly the tragic contrast with the situation as a whole. The Negro lad showed himself painfully aware of the grim realities of contemporary American life, realities from which, with the best intentions in the world, a Fifth Avenue clergyman is somehow far removed. In general, for all the welcome signs of improvement in American race relations in recent years—stemming, incidentally, from the efforts of secular forces primarily, and certainly not from the sort of reassuring and complacent preaching which a man like Peale offers—the fact still remains that it *is* their color that determines how "high Americans go." When we pretend otherwise we are guilty of unconscious duplicity. We maneuver in a world that does not exist. There is much irony in Peale's trying to make an essentially tragic condition vanish by means of a few well-chosen words.

Reinhold Niebuhr remarks that the element of comedy is never completely absent from irony. One hardly needs a college education or very great intelligence to discern in the following piece of advice from *Stay Alive All Your Life* the irony that approaches comedy. Peale lists eleven steps in answer to the question, "how to believe." Almost unbelievably, the first step in its totality reads, "Believe." Our initial reaction to the advice that the way to believe is to believe may well be laughter. But at once we remember that this counsel is offered in complete seriousness and good faith and is apparently received in the same spirit by the multitudes who follow Peale. There is neither good taste nor charity in responding with amusement to the life-and-death assertions and problems of other people. Yet, this does not annul the element of responsibility. The serious fact remains that in more than one place in his writings Peale raises "how to" questions only to answer them by the simple expedient of striking out the two quoted words and then repeating the latter part of the question. Apparently, the way to stop worrying, on the Peale view, is to stop worrying. The extremely worrisome impediment here is that too many people continue to worry even after they have done their best to stop. Few can stop any of their fears and anxieties by the simple device of stopping. One disillusioned woman described her experience with Peale this way: "What he told me, in effect, was that I did not really have a problem." Here is epitomized what many other troubled persons must, in retrospect, have come to feel.

In deference to the comic aspect in irony, the bizarre possibility arises that if we are going to simplify matters so, we may as well follow out that approach to its logical conclusion. The fact that peace of mind piety has to keep toiling and toiling and toiling seems rather odd in light of its own point of view and claim. If human beings possess so much latent strength, why should they not galvanize all their energies right now, sally forth to an unforbidding Armageddon, and conquer all worry in one fell swoop? If anxiety can be overwhelmed by a formula and if there is absolutely no limit to what the human mind can do with its problems,[8] why not engineer a Final Formula right now and get the whole business over with? Life can then be fully and immediately enjoyed. The Final Formula might read, "Conquer *every* problem. Do it *this minute!*" If this Final Formula should prove impossible of application, the cult of reassurance has no choice but to revise its faith that strong men can supply an answer for their every problem. Meanwhile, the constantly reiterated urge to achieve peace, peace, peace when there is no peace remains anything but peaceful. To stop the beating in their ears men may be goaded on to ever more frantic warfare. A statistical-minded friend of Peale once calculated that people in this country suffer from 7.5 billion headaches a year. The question is whether this rate has decreased any as the circulation of Peale's books has increased. The grave, negative thought presents itself that

instead of being a cure for our problems, the cult of reassurance may be no more than a basic symptom and revelation of our plight.

In common with certain other individualistic representations of folk piety, the cult of reassurance has nothing
to offer concerning the whole continuing crisis of our
culture, which greatly exceeds in seriousness a mere 7.5
billion headaches. Most people may appear contented.
Their contentment is not able to conceal certain facts:
the Bomb, the global struggle with communism, the threat
of space warfare, a tragic lack of world community in spite
of the interdependence of the nations, and the peculiar
dilemma which in this country ensnares people between
the norms of competitiveness and of service. In connection
with this last issue, Paul Tillich is right in warning that
the recent upsurge in religion may simply be a means for
the healing of disintegrating personalities so that they can
once more become "good" men in the competitive society.

The crisis of our time helps to produce more distraught
souls than the priests of the cult of reassurance could ever
manage to help. These priests are not unlike Red Cross
workers in wartime, binding up the wounded so that they
can go forth and get shot to pieces all over again.

The Call to Self-Centeredness and Success

There remains at least one further difficulty with the
cult of reassurance in the context of the problem of irony.
This cult presupposes that the great American disease is
anxiety. Are not men assailed, in actuality, by a considerable number of serious mental, moral, and spiritual mala-
dies? These include the disease of self-centeredness, which
the cult of reassurance does not treat but rather seems to

aggravate. It should not come as a surprise that so many people are attracted to this cult. For what is there that concerns us more than ourselves? Reference was made above to the appropriateness of a summons to act where sloth and irresponsibility are present. Yet, it is ironic, if not tragic, to issue a call to action while implicitly denying human responsibility:

> The absence of an understanding of grace, of sin, of the real evil, and of faith in Christian terms, means also that a Christian sense of responsibility is absent. Throughout Peale's multitudinous writings, . . . there is not a single reference to God's righteousness or justice. The prophets are never quoted. To mention God's righteousness would be to make demands upon believers, and Peale's message is not one which makes demands. . . .
>
> The message that there is nothing to feel guilty about goes well with those who do not want to be placed under any claim of responsibility. To regard oneself as bound up in life with men, for whom one has an endless responsibility, would be too much of a negative thought.
>
> . . . One should not indict oneself for one's comfortable and complacent life, for that would not be to believe in oneself. From Peale's message ambitious men receive a boost in getting to what they want, and are taken off the hook of any feeling of guilt toward others, or toward the social order in which they are trying to achieve success.[9]

But it is highly doubtful whether the attraction can endure anyway. The cult of reassurance summons people to happiness through the outgoing life. Yet, the frankly admitted motive remains ulterior. This points to a fatal internal contradiction in the Peale method. How in the world can the self be saved from itself if, essentially, it never gets beyond a concentration upon the problem of its

own salvation? Norman Vincent Peale likes to quote
Jesus' saying that "whoever seeks to gain his life will lose
it, but whoever loses his life will preserve it." It is so easy
for us to stop short here, failing to accept the paradox
in its radical fullness. To the extent that we "lose" our
lives *in order to* find them, we have missed the whole
point. "Seek first the kingdom of God and his righteousness," and, as a byproduct, "all these things shall be yours
as well." "He who loses his life *for my sake* will find it." [10]
Self-fulfillment is an accompaniment of self-surrender; it
can never be the purpose of self-surrender, even a purpose
that has been temporarily removed from consciousness.
Jesus was not supplying a method for achieving psychological well-being; his paradox reveals instead what it is
like to be a member of the kingdom of God. According
to the Christian faith, we reach no final peace apart from
peace with God; yet, peace with God appears only when
we have abandoned the search for our own peace.

The gospel according to Peale reaches its climax in the
promise that anyone who will really put himself to it can
become a *success*. Indeed, one formidable obstacle to a
successful (?) critique of Peale is that Americans are already so imbued with the idea of success as an intrinsic
good that they tend to be preveniently on Peale's side.

What is success? Peale does not reduce success to a
verbal definition, and this probably is wise. Ultimate
values—success, well-being, security, the Good, God—are
usually too grand for mere logical characterization. Practically speaking, success means for Peale, as was quoted
earlier, "the development of mature and constructive personality." To try to define these added terms would simply
worsen the problem of definition. It is, however, an easy
matter to ascertain Peale's objective *criteria* of success. He

supplies them through the many stories and illustrations he uses. His criteria are adopted outright from that side of the American ideal—a secularized version of the Puritan ethic—which praises the accumulation of this world's goods and blessings.

The secular doctrine of evolutionary, upward progress comes in to furnish added incentive. It is not accidental that Peale's writings abound with case histories of men who have "risen" from obscurity to be generals or presidents of huge corporations. The very idea of life as a pilgrimage from the "bottom" to the "top"—there is always room at the top—is an application of the evolutionary theories of Herbert Spencer. In his *Social Statics,* Spencer wrote that "man will eventually become completely suited to his mode of life." Here we have the precursor of the idea of "adjustment" which is so central in the thinking of Peale and others.[11]

All these considerations help to explain, and to make quite logical, an apparent contradiction in Peale's thinking: We should get ahead, and yet we should adjust to the *status quo.* Peale's ideal man is not the Nietzschean Superman who tramples down traditional values, fashioning his own wish-standards as he crashes onward. In Peale, the successful man is the individual who rises to the top all right, but his stairway to the stars is supported by the optimistic, middle-class, competitive system of values within "the American way of life." The successful man is the one who realizes the eminently respectable goals of prosperity, social recognition, and the "fulfillment of his potentialities."

Wayne E. Oates emphasizes that any evaluation of Peale's work must take into account the end objective of the reassurances made.

[Peale] schematizes these reassurances in the direction of success. Successful results are the criteria of everything from prayer
to preaching. This fits into what Karen Horney has called the
competitive neurosis of our times. Here, in this success-religion,
the success pattern of American Business has been given a
religious version. Then, in order that these successful self
physicians may heal themselves, the conditioned reflexes of
ritualistic relaxation are called in to serve as healing formulae.
Hereby he succumbs to the ethical values of optimistic secularism; a real rival to Christianity in any age.[12]

As Pontius Pilate once posed the embarrassingly perennial question, "What is truth?", so we must ask, "What
is success?" We are not looking for a mere definition here;
we want to know whether Peale's successful man is *really*
a success. We want to know where his successful man is.
We want to have a look at this man. This is not "egghead"
theorizing now; we have to keep on asking this sort of
question because it arises from a deep irony in human
experience. It would be very nice if self-fulfillment and
success always lived at peace with one another. Too often,
alas, they stand arrayed in battle. What if the seeker of
success, blessed with the grand "opportunity" to "make
something of himself," only finds himself enmeshed in the
"rat race" of American "people's capitalism"? Just what
is he supposed to do? The question of success forever pur-
sues each one of us, and perhaps most especially those
of us who are "successful." *Is anyone ever a success?* This
is a haunting question. By the very asking of it, success is
forced into a corner. Somehow the luster is already gone.
Unfortunately, human desires are indeterminate. Is it not
sad that the quest for success must be, of its own nature,
unsuccessful? *We face, by contrast, the terrible, saving
eventuality that success is incarnate only in a crucified*

man. Each of us is able to present this eventuality to himself. It is born of our irrepressible imagination. The obsession with success may be seen as an affront to human dignity. For this imagination of ours is indeterminate too. What happens, in sum, when the "successful" man is plagued with the vision of a different order of success? He must remain at any and every moment something of an inevitable failure.

How does the Peale gospel speak to our condition here? One of the more widely voiced critical reactions to Peale is that perhaps without being aware of it, his very treatment of human failure dissociates him from the Christian tradition. Peale tends to be nettled—as probably most of us would be—when the charge is made that his message is suspect from a Christian point of view.[13] In any case, it appears that the problem of irony is again at issue. As finite creatures, are not men supposed to accept their limitations rather than to deny that they have any? Furthermore, there is a decisive sense in which Christianity is a religion of and for failure. The faith that has a Cross at its center knows much of the unavoidable failures of life.

The confrontation of the self as weak, limited, finite, and sinful, as having erred in the nature and direction of its wishes, as having found a Love greater than its own desire, and as having been crucified, buried, and resurrected with that Love —this is not found in Dr. Peale's books.[14]

To fail or to succeed—which is the Christian way? Is the sick-souled individual necessarily in a more evil state than the healthy-minded one? As William James saw a number of years back, not only are the evil facts, which healthy-mindedness fails to account for, a genuine portion of reality; "they may after all be the best key to life's significance, and possibly the only openers of our eyes to the deepest levels of truth." [15]

The primary trouble with happiness seems to be, unhappily, that it does not make us happy. It is a will-o'-the-wisp. It hovers on the edge of self-despair.[16]

Notes

1. Wayne E. Oates, "The Cult of Reassurance," *Religion in Life,* Winter, 1954–1955, pp. 72-82. This article was reprinted from *The Review and Expositor* for July, 1954. The quotations which follow are used by permission of *The Review and Expositor.*

2. In his *Life* article, Paul Hutchinson wonders, appropriately, what the psychiatrists in Peale's church clinic, with their top-flight medical training, must think of their founder-president's preaching.

3. Interestingly enough, we are provided with more than one inkling of negative thinking on Peale's own part. "A rudimentary fact that many miss is that there are some people and things in this world that you just have to get along with, and no amount of resistance or railing will accomplish anything except to increase your frustration. Therefore, the quiet and urbane philosophy of accepting persons and situations, and of learning to think about them peacefully, is most important in eliminating frustrated feelings." (From p. 48, *Stay Alive All Your Life* by Norman Vincent Peale, copyright 1957 by Prentice-Hall, Inc., published by Prentice-Hall, Inc., Englewood Cliffs, N. J.) Peale is not always entirely consistent with his highly voluntaristic philosophy.

4. Quoted in *Time,* Nov. 1, 1954, p. 68.

5. Some will find a passage in an earlier volume by Peale (*The Power of Positive Thinking*) that is much more directed to their condition: "Collapse physically. Practice this several times a day." Many people can do *that* all right, with little or no effort, and

without benefit of either clergy or bootstraps. But, seriously, the rapid-fire alternation in Peale's counsel between doing everything and refraining from doing anything leaves one rather bewildered. It is somewhat reminiscent of the cycle in which the manic-depressive personality is caught: world-conquering action alternating with withdrawal from the world.

6. From *Stay Alive All Your Life* by Norman Vincent Peale (© 1957 by Prentice-Hall, Inc., published by Prentice-Hall, Inc., Englewood Cliffs, N.J.), pp. 95-96.

7. *Ibid.*

8. With the help of God.

9. William Lee Miller, "The Gospel of Norman Vincent Peale," *Union Seminary Quarterly Review*, Jan., 1955, pp. 19-20. By permission of *Union Seminary Quarterly Review*.

10. Matthew 6:33; 10:39.

11. Francis J. Trembley, a biologist friend of the writer, has pointed out that the notion of adjustment is in an important respect very bad advice from an evolutionary point of view. The creature that adjusts, dies; only the creative organism endures.

12. Wayne E. Oates, "The Cult of Reassurance," *Religion in Life*, Winter, 1954–1955, p. 81. This article was reprinted from *The Review and Expositor*, July, 1954. Used by permission of *The Review and Expositor*.

13. "Criticism that [his] is a truncated theology and a psychology so oversimplified that in the long run it may do more harm than good will not deter [Norman Vincent Peale]. He apparently has no worries at all about what his theology is, beyond a reiteration of the simple evangelical formulas of his boyhood. He can match any report of psychological harm wrought with a dozen testimonials from grateful disciples. Criticism that he harps on only one string he can shrug off. What is successful advertising but endless repetition of a single slogan? And the response to the Peale formula has been so great that—despite criticism which he knows exists and which I think distresses him, for he is a reasonably humble and sensitive man—little Peales are sprouting in clerical ranks all over the country." (From Paul Hutchinson,

"Have We a 'New' Religion?", *Life,* Apr. 11, 1955, p. 157. By permission of the copyright owner, Agnes M. Hutchinson.)

14. Oates, *op. cit.,* pp. 77, 78.

15. William James, *The Varieties of Religious Experience* (New York: Random House, Modern Library Edition, 1902), p. 160.

16. For fuller presentations of a religio-psychological point of view from which the cult of reassurance may be evaluated, consult two full-length studies by Wayne E. Oates: *Religious Factors in Mental Illness* (New York: Association Press, 1955), and *Religious Dimensions of Personality* (New York: Association Press, 1957).

Chapter : FIVE

Irony and the Revival of Revivalism

We consider next the problem of ironic strains within the resurgent revivalism of the day.[1]

An analytical difficulty is involved here, somewhat related to one that was raised in Chapter One and again in Chapter Two—the dual problem of comprehending religion in general terms and in particular terms. Revivalism as a general evangelistic method goes back some two centuries. To offer a generalized critique of revivalism as a historical movement would take us too far afield. Our interest here is specifically in the contemporary situation. On the other hand, we cannot avoid the fact that the new revivalism continues many of the aspects of the old revivalism. As we consider the present scene we cannot ignore continuing problems posed by the revivalist approach as a whole.

The Billy Graham campaigns have done more than anything else to bring about the marked revival of revivalism in our day. If Norman Vincent Peale is the high priest of the cult of reassurance, Billy Graham is the ablest apostle of the new revivalism. We shall proceed through specific reference to the Graham enterprise. Should the Grahamites' strength contain hidden weaknesses and their wisdom conceal folly, the eventuality of irony is close at hand. This eventuality becomes apparent at several points.

The Evangelist and the Holy Adversary

The avowed purpose of the new revivalism is "to bring men to Christ." The revivalists make the strong claim that they are able to fulfill this purpose and, indeed, that they have been uniquely commissioned by the Lord to this end.

It is our contention that the issue of numbers of "converts" or "inquirers" is not *in itself* a crucial means of judging the Graham enterprise. True, there is considerable doubt of the overt successes of the Grahamites in this area, as a recent appraisal by *The New York Times* of the 1957 New York crusade has to a limited extent shown.[2] On the other hand, it is ridiculous to deny that some men are in some way "brought to Christ" through the ministry of religious revivalists. Only the prejudiced will refuse to grant that of an imagined total, a good proportion of conversions will endure. Even if the final number proved minimal, the effort would not thereby be unjustified. Faith is debased when it is subjected to quantitative criteria of success. Thus, Billy Graham was, from one point of view, absolutely right when he responded to *The New York Times*' study by saying that "if one person's life was changed during the crusade, it would have been well worth the entire effort."

The problem of irony is introduced at two points. First, the role that Graham occupies is more than that of merely another evangelist. Comments such as the one just quoted cannot be finally appraised in isolation from Graham's responsibilities as head of a vast organization which expends huge sums of money and consumes the energies and time of countless individuals. It is hard to treat the comment above on its face value when it comes from a man in Graham's position. Could the organization men of the Graham enterprise ever be prepared to settle for one conversion? These men have learned to implement Norman Vincent Peale's advice to "think big, believe big, pray big, act big" and to "think success, believe in success, and visualize success," in a way that must "set in motion the powerful force of the realizable wish." An evangelist of a humble Christian mission in a remote section of rural India could, after a lifetime of work, offer a comment like Graham's and there would be a certain glory and rationality in it. When Graham makes such a comment, the lights of Madison Square Garden are there to expose its artificiality. In the Indian evangelist the weakness of the statement would be its strength; in Graham the strength of the statement becomes its weakness. The Grahamites are defeated by their own mathematics. Quality is taken captive by quantity. If *one* person's life is the treasure that really counts, the question is inescapable: *Why this kind of effort?*

Second, although Billy Graham's genuine and sincere contriteness helps somewhat to offset the pretensions of his claims, that contriteness is not strong enough to make him ask himself whether it may have been the Holy Spirit rather than the Devil who on one occasion made off with his sermon notes designed for the winning of souls.[3] The text, "He who sits in the heavens laughs; the Lord has them in derision," [4] is a good one for any preacher to use, but Graham cannot apply this particular text to his own efforts. The thought that the Lord could possibly be standing in judgment upon this whole technique for conversion is unbearable and must not be admitted to consciousness. For, after all, was not Madison Square Garden the *Lord's* idea?

The new revivalism rightly condemns the idolatries and blasphemies of contemporary men, but it maintains its own presumptions against the Holy Spirit. As indicated in Chapter Two, Billy Graham's Christian position in part places him outside folk religion. Nevertheless, like most more orthodox adherents of folk religion, Graham is absolutely convinced that God is working through him and his enterprise. It would probably be well for him spiritually, and, therefore, helpful to countless other people, if he were to doubt this once in a while.

The issue here extends beyond personal character into the very procedures of mass evangelism in their contemporary form. To quote from a *Christian Century* editorial on Graham's Madison Square Garden campaign,

The most serious challenge to Billy Graham and all his aiders and abetters comes not from disdainful liberals or from frightened fundamentalists but from Christians at the strong center of the church who sense a certain blasphemy in all this red-hot machinery and cool contrivance. Our objections are no longer the usual sober ones against older, pneumatic evangelism: that it depended too casually and too confidently on the docile presence of the Holy Spirit. Our objections now are to the Graham procedure which does its mechanical best to "succeed" whether or not the Holy Spirit is in attendance. At this strange new junction of Madison Avenue and Bible Belt, the Holy Spirit is not overworked; he is overlooked.

... Prayerful and humble as Billy Graham is, his plans and his methods show no faith in the caprice of the Holy Spirit, have no leeway for the wind that blows where it wills. ...

Maybe the appropriate measure in all this is the possibility of failure. We are actually missing the possibility of failure. There is something horrifying in this monstrous juggernaut rolling over every sensitivity to its sure triumph. If only there were a chance it might have failed, how much more hope the church might have had from its success. If only there were something more real for Him to do, how much more at home the Spirit might have been in the Garden.[5]

Something will be added later on concerning this matter of failure and success. Perhaps the Holy Spirit did have something to do after all.[6]

Attraction and Repulsion

The Graham version of the gospel attracts many people. How many does it repel?

The Christian gospel means good news. It is not primarily a new demand. It is deliverance. One comes away from hearing Billy Graham wondering how much the preacher knows this. In ways not a little reminiscent of the self-demanding emphases in Norman Vincent Peale's preaching, Graham stresses the onerous necessity for men to *do* something before it is too late. Much in Graham's entire procedure builds up to an either-or decision that may be more terror than salvation. In the vein of the modern existentialists, the stress falls on crisis. Attention to sin and repentance is, of course, constituent to the total Christian message. Graham's insistence upon the element of self-abnegation in Christian faith makes his point of view much more biblical than Peale's. The question is one of balance. Graham's gospel message could do with more of the exultation that the cult of reassurance seeks, however scarcely it finds it.

Neither Graham nor Peale seems to have much comprehension of the Christian paradox of the demand that is at once a divine gift. This paradox is embodied in the teaching of Jesus. In many places Jesus stresses the absolute demands of God. Men are to love God with all their heart, mind, soul, and strength. But if God's demands are absolute, his love is infinite. "The God who asks everything is eager also to give everything." He forgives to the uttermost. He is a God of grace as well as of moral truth.[7]

It is a pity when the bad news about human frailty and despair contravenes the good news of God's answer. Men may thus be driven into the anguish which the Christian gospel, on its own terms, can actually overcome. They may, for that matter, be driven into the cult of reassurance, where they will imagine, for a time at least, that they can attain acceptance as human beings.

In Graham's preaching one is not impressed with the great joy that radiates through the New Testament. The early Christians were able to be joyous because of their experience that beyond all demand lies the final Power who accepts men not just when they repent—how like human *eros* that would be!—but when they do nothing to merit acceptance. To become a Christian is not a calculating device for avoiding the descent into hell or for gaining ascent into heaven. To become a Christian means joyous gratefulness to the Being who ever seeks out the sheep which is lost.

The great contrast between a religion of demand and a faith of deliverance is illustrated in a childlike, powerful sermon of Paul Tillich based on the word of Jesus, "Come unto me, all ye that labor and are heavy laden, and I will give you rest . . . my yoke is easy and my burden is light."

Taking upon oneself His easy yoke does not mean taking sin more easily or taking guilt less seriously. He does not tell those who come to Him that their sins are not so important as they seemed to be. He does not give them an easier conscience about their failures. . . .

What Jesus does is to take from men the burden of religion:

The religious law demands that [a man] accept ideas and dogmas, that he believe in doctrines and traditions, the acceptance of which is the condition of his salvation from anxiety, despair and death. So he tries to accept them, although they may have become strange or doubtful to him. He labors and toils under the religious demand to believe things he cannot believe. . . .

The same is true of the practical laws of religion. They demand ritual activities, the participation in religious enterprises, and the study of religious traditions, prayer, sacraments and meditations. They demand moral obedience, inhuman self-control and asceticism, devotion to man and things beyond our possibilities, surrender to ideas and duties beyond our power, unlimited self-negation, and unlimited self-perfection: the religious law demands the perfect in all respects. . . .

. . . The yoke of Jesus . . . is not a new demand, a new doctrine or new morals, but rather a new reality, a new being and a new power of transforming life. He calls it a yoke, He means that it comes from above and grasps us with saving force; if He calls it easy, He means that it is not a matter of our acting and striving, but rather that it is given before anything we can do. It is being, power, reality, conquering the anxiety and despair, the fear and the restlessness of our existence. . . .

. . . Forget all Christian doctrines; forget your own certainties and your own doubts, when you hear the call of Jesus. Forget all Christian morals, your achievements and your failures, when you come to Him. Nothing is demanded of you— not your being religious, not your being Christian, not your being wise, and not your being moral. But what is demanded is only your being open and willing to accept what is given to you, the New Being, the being of love and justice and truth, as it is manifest in Him Whose yoke is easy and Whose burden is light. . . .[8]

The love that God possesses is an ultimate resource beyond the divine judgment; in the Graham message it almost seems as though the divine love must work especially hard to keep pace with the divine judgment.

Perhaps it is not irreverent to repeat the old tale of the man who was asked by a stranger while riding in a bus (it always seems to be a bus), "Have you found the Savior?" He answered, "I hadn't heard that he was lost." Much of our modern revivalism faces the temptation of the ancient Pelagian heresy in the Church, the fancy that men somehow determine their eternal salvation by their own decision of will. Resemblance to the preaching of Norman Vincent Peale is again apparent. What is not so apparent is resemblance to the peace of God that surpasses all human powers.

Many people step forward to be counted at the preacher's invitation. What of those who do not? Is irresponsibility the only cause? Or personal intransigence? Or the absence of the Holy Spirit? A live possibility is honest alienation induced by the preacher's message itself. Perhaps more than one person relives the story of the rich young man who "went away sorrowful" rather than staying to hear Jesus' answer to the disciples' question of how *anybody* can be saved: "With men it is impossible, but

not with God; for all things are possible with God." [9] Can
Christian preaching flaunt human integrity? Did not Jesus
come that men "may have life, and have it abundantly"? [10]

An Easy Answer

The onerous character of the preacher's demand is
matched by the ease of the solution. The irony of simplification is a decisive eventuality within the gospel according to Billy Graham.

For example, Graham has lamented that "a generation
ago we took God out of our educational system." Apart
from the fact that it would be quite a feat if human beings
could take God out of anything, Graham's diagnosis almost
appears to suggest its own remedy: "How stupid of us!
Let's put God back!" God is important, education is good,
education would be much better if God were there, et
cetera, et cetera. Thus do men go from simplicity to simplicity.

In his narrative history of Protestantism in America,
Jerald C. Brauer offers a statement which, though directed
to the revivalism of the frontier, remains pertinent today:

Because revivalism reduced everything to a matter of simple
choice—Christ or the devil, sin or goodness, infidelity or faith—
it both answered the needs of western people and made it very
difficult for them to pass on to a deeper understanding of the
religious life. Faith was not always a simple matter of choice.
One's whole past life formed one's decisions. To be sure, under
the great emotional stimulus of the camp meeting one might
be able to break through the past and to decide for God. But
what happened when the emotional appeal was not present?

Simplifying the issues through emotional appeals made
choices easier, but it overlooked many basic problems. It ig-

nored the responsibility of the Christian faith to address current intellectual difficulties. It centered only on moral results. The consequence was that it was extremely successful in meeting the needs of the frontier, but it produced a spirit in American Christianity that made it difficult for Christianity to shift its emphasis in the face of new frontiers.[11]

Typical of this simplifying of issues is Billy Graham's declaration that "every human problem can be solved and every hunger satisfied and every potential can be fulfilled when a man encounters Jesus Christ and comes in vital relation to God in him." Reinhold Niebuhr, who concedes that Graham is better than any previous American evangelist of his kind, points out, nevertheless, that the success of such mass revivalism is dependent upon oversimplifying every issue of life.

Perhaps because these solutions are rather too simple in any age, but particularly so in a nuclear one with its great moral perplexities, such a message is not very convincing to anyone —Christian or not—who is aware of the continual possibilities of good and evil in every advance of civilization, every discipline of culture, and every religious convention. Graham offers Christian evangelism even less complicated answers than it has ever before provided. . . .

. . . [He] promises a new life, not through painful religious experience but merely by signing a decision card. Thus, a miracle of regeneration is promised at a painless price by an obviously sincere evangelist. It is a bargain.[12]

W. Burnet Easton, Jr., himself a perennial critic of sentimentality in religion, has recently expressed certain doubts that bear upon the issue of oversimplification. Easton raises no question about the vital importance of intellectuality within the Christian church or about the contribution of men like Reinhold and Richard Niebuhr and Paul Tillich. But what is it that intellectuals tend to do? They presuppose

a willingness and an ability to analyze all situations profoundly and to undergo the agony of uncertainty about what to do in the next situation and the agony of facing endless decisions. This is too much to expect from most people. T. S. Eliot may be a bit of an intellectual snob, but there is some truth in his remark that humankind "cannot bear very much reality." I suspect it is too much for most intellectuals too, but certainly average laymen and laywomen are not constantly interested in paradoxical ambiguities. They want, desperately, certain absolutes, or at least working standards, around which they can organize their lives. What have we to tell them?
. . . In our honest desire to be realistic and to avoid oversimplification of the very real complexities of life, are we tending to a new idolatry which can end in moral nihilism? [13]

As far as the Graham evangelistic enterprise is concerned, it is difficult, so Easton says, to escape the conclusion that Billy Graham mediates the grace of God to many people in ways that the intellectual could never do. Perhaps, therefore, Graham's "greatest contribution will be what his success says to Christian intellectuals."

In effect, what Easton sees, shrewdly, is that the fear of oversimplification can conceivably prove to be too simple an understanding! His comments help to bring home the truth that possible insight into the ineffectuality of others does not in itself make a man any less ineffectual at the practical level. Nevertheless, as indicated early in Chapter Three, the problem of oversimplification has to be met, not primarily on the basis of that criterion as an abstract principle, but on a rather different basis: Does a particular strategy under examination succeed, on its own terms, in accomplishing something substantial and enduring? Does Graham's preaching in fact implement the Christian faith or does it impede that faith? In the nature of the case, no one can furnish a categorical reply to this latter question.

We can proceed, nevertheless, on the ground of simple logic. Should a good many of the people ostensibly reached by Graham fail to go on to a vital faith and should Graham's analysis of our social plight fail to merit support by experience, then, in this particular respect, roles are reversed. Graham's position becomes the impractical one and the position opposed to his becomes the one that must make sense to "average laymen." The Graham solution is so sweeping that it supposedly takes care not alone of individual spiritual problems but of the world's problems as well. John C. Bennett has referred to an illusion in Graham's point of view which pervades the whole revivalist tradition—the illusion that somehow the nation as a whole can escape corporate disaster if only enough people repent of their personal sins as individuals.[14] It would seem—and we speak from some experience here—that more than one New York City taxi driver knows from "bearing" quite a little "reality" that the revivalist is the one who lives in a dream world.[15] We should not have to search far to find a taxi driver prepared to testify that the intercontinental missiles would not be deterred from falling by the repentance of a mere one hundred million people.

Whether the new revivalists please such Christian intellectuals as have a constitutional aversion to simplification is, in consequence, quite irrelevant. There is the simplicity that, in oversimplifying, is irresponsible and there is also the simple insight that knows the unreality in such oversimplification.

The New Fundamentalism

Additional raw material for irony is provided by the
fact that Billy Graham's interpretation of Scripture is
fundamentalist. He subscribes to the basic doctrines of
the fundamentalist creed. These include the virgin birth
of Jesus, the literal infallibility of the Bible, the substi-
tutionary blood atonement of Christ, and the literal and
imminent second coming of Christ. From the standpoint
of fundamentalism, these tenets furnish a standard for
determining what is orthodox and, indeed, make up the
essence of Christian faith.

The controversy between representatives of religious
faith and advocates of science and scientific evolutionism
has for the most part subsided in this country. Though
part of the responsibility lay with dogmatists in science
and apostles of modern cultural norms, much of the fault
lay too with a militant fundamentalism which, in effect,
turned the Bible into an inerrant textbook.[16] We presume
that the majority of thinking Christians today see the
Bible as *containing* the Word of God but not in a literal
or inerrant sense and not in the extraneous sense of com-
petition with scientific treatises. A truly evangelical understanding of Christian faith, though not necessarily contra-
dicting all the basic doctrines of fundamentalism, will,
nevertheless, deny that only those are fundamental.[17]

In a review of the inexpensive edition of Graham's
book, *Peace with God,* Theodore A. Gill writes:

If this is a fair sample of the Graham evangelism, then I do
not know how we shall ever repair its damage. Such preaching
alienates the core of the society it tries to bring to God. Among
the creators of our culture too many already think that the

gospel is obscurantist, anti-intellectual nonsense with nothing to offer the thinkers and the planners and the doers. Then, in the full blare of publicity to which the churches contribute, Dr. Graham confirms them in their negative impression. It is heart-breaking to think what he has done to undo the patient, suggestive, creative interpreting of the gospel which has begun to commend it to those who could most imaginatively amplify and implement it.[18]

We do not imply that scientific or modern cultural criteria are the judges of religious affirmations. The Christian gospel has a standing ground that is independent of any prevailing culture. The real issue is whether, in its task of evangelism, the Church ought to become involved once again in artificial opposition between the religious and the scientific approaches to life. The evangelizing task of the Church would receive a severe setback. How unfortunate it would be if a battle once won—largely through the contribution of modern historical scholarship on the part of Christian thinkers—had to be refought. Irony would reap the victory. For the wisdom of biblical faith becomes folly when it does not know that its treasure is "in earthen vessels, to show that the transcendent power belongs to God and not to us." [19] The Christian gospel may be largely a stumbling block to modern culture, but, if we must fight, let us at least wage fresh battles.

A more serious problem is involved here than that of a renewing of the controversy between representatives of science and of religion. Will Herberg has suggested the need for a distinction between scholastic fundamentalism and pietistic fundamentalism. The former, doctrinal type has not been terribly influential in very recent religious circles. The latter is much more widespread. Pietistic fundamentalism, as Reinhold Niebuhr has expressed it, "reduces the faith to a simple panacea for all the ills of the world. . . . It solves all problems of life by asking bad people to become good and to prove it by loving one another." [20]

With Billy Graham, pietistic fundamentalism overshadows any concern for doctrinal niceties. Graham is, ironically enough, reintroducing the illusions of an earlier Christian utopianism which had actually succeeded in emancipating itself from the type of uncritical biblicism that Graham represents. We have had fundamentalists who have told us that if only we will believe in the Word of God, our eternal salvation is achieved. And we have had utopians who have counseled that if only men will just love one another, peace for the world is assured. But it has been left to the Billy Graham enterprise to put the two sides together on an unprecedented scale, through powerful assistance from modern advertising methods and the mass media. Thus, Graham does not merely proclaim to the world that through faith *man can solve all his problems;* he supports this assurance with the magic words, *The Bible says so.*[21] The combination could not be more ominous. For no combination could contribute more to the futility of an alleged Christian message in these troublous times. It is here that irony is transmuted into potential tragedy for the American people and perhaps for all men. The world cries for spiritual food only to receive the stone of an inerrant book; the world cries for moral succor only to be tempted by the serpent of perfectionism. The possession of illusions is the surest guide to failure in seeking "proximate solutions for all the insoluble problems of our collective life, problems that are constantly growing in dimension in a technical age." [22]

Revivalism and the Church

In continuation of a previous point about the contending of Billy Graham with the Holy Spirit, it must be made plain that the Graham enterprise bears a conspicuously equivocal relation to the historic Christian community. In this we are reminded of traditional revivalist attitudes. There is also a point of contact here with certain other forms of the surging American piety.

It cannot be claimed that the Church is divine. The Holy Spirit does indeed have its own caprice. Yet, the persons of the Christian Trinity stand in close relation. The Church is the Body of Christ and, unless it turn traitor to its Lord, Christians can anticipate that the Holy Spirit will continue to live in the Church.

In his book, *Peace with God,* Billy Graham includes a chapter on "The Christian and the Church." On the face of it, his doctrine of the Church is an exalted one. The Church is the *ecclesia,* the called-out people of God. Its purpose is to glorify God, build human fellowship, strengthen faith, channel Christian stewardship, spread the gospel, and implement Christian service and humanitarianism. The thousand and one tasks that are to be done for Christ "can best be accomplished through the fellowship of a local church. . . . The church is the organization of Christ upon earth." [23]

In the light of Graham's exalted view of the Church as here expressed—although the first part of the quotation just given reflects his Baptist presuppositions—and in the light also of the established practice of the Graham forces to refer "inquirers" to local clergymen, it is noteworthy that Graham should also express sentiments opposite to those mentioned. His reservations are not those of the erstwhile supporter who comes to turn against the Church through a conviction that it has become un-Christian. Graham recognizes the many shortcomings and evils of the Church, but he does not let these annul his relatively exalted point of view. Nevertheless, on the occasion of the altar calls in his revival services we hear Graham offering again and again a word of counsel which closely parallels this statement of purpose from the beginning of *Peace with God*:

My object is not to get you to a particular denomination or church—but to get you to a saving knowledge of the Lord Jesus Christ, and to encourage, strengthen, and build up the Christian in the most holy faith.[24]

This is ambivalent counsel. If it means that the evangelist has no axe to grind for one denomination above others, that is one thing. The problem remains of how the individual can receive saving knowledge of Christ, together with needed encouragement, strength, and nurture, except through *some* denomination and church. Neither Billy Graham's book nor his preaching can do it. Growth in grace is a slow and often painful process. The ministry of the fellowship of believers is indispensable.

All this points to a related difficulty in mass evangelism as a whole. There is a tremendous contrast between a great revival meeting and a service in the little church over on Fourth Street. Inevitably, the new believer, or even the old believer, must feel something of a spiritual letdown when he takes up with the necessarily more prosaic life of his local congregation. This point is hardly a convincing argument against mass evangelism as such. In any area of life, for men to avoid the heights of experience simply because they must spend most of their time in the straight places is a good way for them to turn into dullards. Nevertheless, when the mass evangelists fold their great tents and glamorously steal away, they remain a party to the problem. For all their disposition to put the onus on supposedly unrevived churches, responsibility still follows after these leaders. A letdown is a letdown only by virtue of its opposite. The sobering thought is that the opposite may have been an emotional jag as much as a confrontation by the Holy Spirit.

Once again *The Christian Century* editors have expressed a compelling reaction:

> . . . Churchmen not under the influence of revivalistic fever know . . . that conversion can be a valid and helpful step in spiritual development only when it is preceded and succeeded by action by the church, not just temporally, but organically. The action of the church is not stuck on the front or tacked on the back of "real" conversion. It is of a piece with that decision, or else the decision itself is isolated, insulated, insignificant.

The new life which should begin at conversion cannot endure very long in isolation; yet isolation is almost inevitable under the circumstances of a Graham crusade. The crusade is set up by outside specialists, is conducted by strangers to the life of the churches in an atmosphere foreign to the churches, is ended in a bookkeeping shuffle to the churches of cards bearing names and addresses of converts. If adoption agencies distributed orphans to foster homes with the insouciance and lack of responsibility revivalists use in scattering neophytes among churches, they would be indicted for inhumanity. . . .

. . . Even with the best will in the world Graham cannot find a more important place in his theology for the church than the simple idea that it is the divinely appointed conservator for converts. So he rejected by silence Reinhold Niebuhr's friendly plea that he help Christians apply the love commandment in relation to just one of the contemporary denials of God's love in our society—the race question. Action along the line Niebuhr suggested would have led Graham into the fellowship of the divinely committed society which is engaged in the endless struggles of the Kingdom of God consolidating itself. It would have made him one with the church in the only way anyone is ever of the church: by participation in the church's service in the world. To stay out so himself, to act as if this were something somehow "added to" conversion instead of the essence and reality of the changed and changing life—this faults the whole crusade. . . .[25]

The Futility of It All

The paragraph last quoted directs us forcibly to a point of equal seriousness with the previous point. As implied in the discussion of the new fundamentalism, our surging revivalism reveals a poignant futility before the frontier issues of our time. Revivalism is tempted to pass by on the other side as the agonies of the world lie untended in the road.

The 1957 New York crusade of the Graham forces stands as a telling symbol of the futility of the new revivalism. A primary, announced objective of that crusade was to reach the unredeemed of the world's greatest—and allegedly most sinful—metropolis in such a way that the forces of evil everywhere would be brought to bay. Accordingly, the new David came trumpeting into the city to wage battle with Goliath. A momentous blow for the Lord was to be struck at, of all places, the very headquarters of the world's wickedness. This would be a sign which every lesser city would ignore at its peril. The shot from David's sling would be heard round the world.

Two things happened that David evidently had not

expected. (Irony always involves the unanticipated.) First, Goliath yawned. *Goliath yawned!* The theatrical journal *Variety,* conveying to its readers that the Graham meetings would be pleasant and inoffensive, proved shrewder than Graham when it commented that if there was anything New Yorkers wanted to be delivered from it was Big Boredom rather than Big Sin. And Billy Graham failed them. Not because Goliath's forces were too confirmed in their sins. (Who is not?) He failed them simply because he was irrelevant. He was interesting, yes, but at the end he too was boring. Unlike the Goliath of history, the modern Goliath did not disdain David. Instead, he did not even have the decency to show up for the fight. Perhaps from out of some recess of his thick head he remembered having learned in childhood that "the blood of the martyrs is the seed of the Church." Goliath could have girded for battle or he could have fled. He did neither. He just yawned.

Second, David's camp followers kept stumbling on to the hoped-for battleground, getting in the way of the theoretically primary contenders. In fact, their presence was one of the things that helped to keep Goliath yawning. Thus, when a special altercation was arranged at a scene traditionally reserved for somewhat different types of slugfest, Yankee Stadium, with no less than 100,000 souls (and bodies) in attendance, it

was the simple, staid, sure, saved of the retrogressive churches who held the field. In the very city where real evangelism depends upon a church eager to be ahead of itself, Protestantism has identified itself officially with the settled-down, sewed-up sanctity of good people who look steadfastly back to a world that is no more. The church did not meet the world at the stadium. The church met itself—its most comfortable, confident

self. Convinced Christians convinced convinced Christians.
And the glow of convictions and prejudices reinforcing each
other was a warm and lovely thing.

But it wasn't evangelism. . . .[26]

Warfare with the unregenerate was transformed peacefully and delightfully into a great rally of the hosts of the
Lord. And everybody seemed supremely happy. Meanwhile, Goliath had turned over and gone to sleep. Then
the campaign was extended by a number of weeks. Was
this because Goliath had at last been awakened and goaded
to fight? Not at all. The Graham forces had experienced
something of the bewilderment that comes from preparing
earnestly for battle and then being unable to establish
contact with the enemy. Meanwhile, the multitudes of the
faithful kept clamoring for attention.

There was little pathos in the regrettable failure of this
central aspect of the Graham purpose in New York City,
and there was little tragedy. Pathos and tragedy are absent
when the claimants are responsible and when the weakness in their great claims is unconscious. The New York
failure was ironic. It was a failure when interpreted from
the side of its own expressed method and point of view.
For the outsider, intangible achievement might suffice. But
for the Grahamites, because of the very nature of their
campaigns and their claims, tangible evidence must remain a decisive consideration. Thus are they vanquished
by their own criteria. *They* said that Goliath was in for
the battle of his life. And the battle never came off. Goliath himself, the abysmal "immoral society" behind and
beyond every "moral man," went his bored and very piti-
able way.

As this is written, there are no signs of soul searching
within the ranks of the new evangelists. Perhaps it is too

early to determine whether contrition or evil will win. Perhaps only a continuing irony can prevent the victory of evil. This irony involves the truth that successful young men can hardly ever admit their irrelevancies and failures, even to themselves and even when their own criteria of faith and action stand arrayed against them.

None of us has any ground for self-righteousness here. Many modern men consider the Christian church as a whole to be largely irrelevant—which means, more precisely, that they hardly consider the Church. Perhaps the Church and its clergy are always boring to the unregenerate (as well as to many who claim to be regenerate). But there is all the difference in the world between acknowledging this fact and proving via the pretentiousness of our claims how unaware we are of our true situation.

Implicit in this discussion of the new revivalism is the persuasion that instead of condemning the movement thoughtlessly, we ought, first, accept it as a genuine attempt to bring the Christian faith to men and, second, make plain its limitations and dangers. Whenever revivalism claims, in effect, that its approach to, and version of, the gospel represent the central core of the Christian evangel, with other approaches either subsidiary or erroneous, we have no alternative but to speak out in criticism. That this type of claim is an integral part of the Billy Graham campaigns makes especially regrettable the support provided by the Protestant Council of New York City of the 1957 crusade in Madison Square Garden. That scheduled delegations from more than 1500 churches appeared at the evening meetings is a sobering commentary upon the so-called "Protestantism" of the churches. It may be that the real irony of the New York crusade transcends the Graham enterprise as such. Perhaps it lies in the fact that so many churches and clergy, either through silence or positive support, allowed the world to believe that fundamentalist evangelism can legitimately and even providentially represent the witness of the Christian church to this generation.

The issue finally turns on whether Christians and the Christian churches are doing anything about their irrelevancies and futilities. "Is it nothing to you, all you who pass by?" [27] Or does the Christian community stop along the road, seeking to bind up the wounds of the agonized whose name is Legion? [28]

Notes

1. "Revivalism" is referred to here in its somewhat limited or technical meaning, as the word is used adjectivally in the phrase "revival meeting," rather than in the more general sense of a "revival of religion." Revivalism may, of course, have a place in a given revival or renascence of religious faith.

2. In its issue of Jan. 26, 1958, *The New York Times* reported results of a poll it had taken of New York ministers concerning the results of the 1957 crusade in that city. Replies were received from 159 ministers, more than a third of those polled. The clergymen were asked to evaluate the crusade and to answer these questions: How many referrals did you receive? How many of these were new names? How many of the referrals are now attending services regularly? Of 3,997 referrals reported, 2,552 had already been church members. Information was inconclusive on the third question, but the *Times* editor indicated that sufficient replies were received to show that "pillars of the church stayed on, but many of the new names went to another church or dropped out of sight." Comments helped to make it evident that most people who went to the Garden rallies were already church members. The *Times* editor pointed out that most of the re-

spondents considered the crusade a failure as an evangelistic effort.

3. Graham reports that one day, when he was preparing a sermon on the Devil for the Madison Square Garden crusade, his notes were mysteriously lost. "One thing was certain—the Devil didn't want me to invade his domain that night!" (From "Why I Believe in the Devil," *This Week* Magazine, March 2, 1958, p. 17. Reprinted from *This Week* Magazine. Copyright 1958 by the United Newspapers Magazine Corporation. Used by permission of Dr. Billy Graham.)

4. Psalms 2:4 (RSV).

5. Editorial, "In the Garden," *The Christian Century*, May 15, 1957, pp. 614-615. Copyright 1957, Christian Century Foundation. Reprinted by permission from *The Christian Century*.

6. See the section below entitled The Futility of It All.

7. John Knox, *The Man Christ Jesus* (Chicago: Willett, Clark & Company, 1942), pp. 42-44.

8. Paul Tillich, "The Yoke of Religion," in *The Shaking of the Foundations* (New York: Charles Scribner's Sons, 1948), pp. 95, 97, 98, 99, 102. By permission of the publishers.

9. See Mark 10:17-27 (RSV).

10. John 10:10 (RSV).

11. From *Protestantism in America* by Jerald C. Brauer. Copyright, 1953, by W. L. Jenkins, The Westminster Press. Used by permission. Pages 113-114.

12. Reinhold Niebuhr in a commentary in *Life*, July 1, 1957, p. 92. By permission of Reinhold Niebuhr.

13. W. Burnet Easton, Jr., "Ethical Relativism and Popular Morality," *Theology Today*, Jan., 1958, pp. 470-477. By permission of *Theology Today*.

14. Bennett, "Billy Graham at Union," *Union Seminary Quarterly Review*, May, 1954, p. 12.

15. The reaction here parallels the plausible response to counsel that the way to stop worrying is to stop.

16. See the account by Harry Emerson Fosdick in *The Living of These Days: An Autobiography* (New York: Harper & Brothers, 1956), Chapter Seven—"The Fundamentalist Controversy."

17. Editorial, "Fundamentalist Revival," *The Christian Century*, June 19, 1957, p. 750.

18. *The Christian Century*, March 23, 1955, p. 369. Copyright 1955, Christian Century Foundation. Reprinted by permission from *The Christian Century*.

19. II Corinthians 4:7 (RSV).

20. Reinhold Niebuhr, "After Comment, the Deluge," *The Christian Century*, September 4, 1957, p. 1035.

21. The impossibility of bringing together in a wholly consistent way utopian expectations and a certain form of biblical literalism is illustrated in Graham's belief in a personal Devil. Graham's insistence that the encounter with Christ solves every human problem contrasts with this foreboding statement: "If we for one moment dare to believe that 'peace in our time' is drawing closer —overnight misunderstanding, suspicion, and ill-will break out afresh. For Satan is determined that the dark, joyless river of humanity shall continue on its tormented way until the end of time." (Billy Graham, "Why I Believe in the Devil," *op. cit.*, p. 18.)

 It is only when we are set free from such biblicism and also from utopian readings of the Bible that we can affirm simultaneously that there is some ground for moral and social advance but that men cannot fashion a perfect society. In the biblical understanding, man remains a sinner but he is also a responsible being whose life can be transformed through the grace of a sovereign and loving God. Billy Graham does not have this dialectical understanding.

22. Reinhold Niebuhr, *op. cit.*, p. 1035.

23. Graham, *Peace with God*, pp. 174, 178-185.

24. From *Peace with God* by Billy Graham, p. 7. Copyright 1953 by Billy Graham, reprinted by permission of Doubleday & Company, Inc.

25. Editorial, "Mass Conversions," *The Christian Century*, May 29, 1957, pp. 678, 679. Copyright 1957, Christian Century Foundation. Reprinted by permission from *The Christian Century*.

26. Editorial, "The Long Anticlimax," *The Christian Century*, Aug. 7, 1957, p. 933. Copyright 1957, Christian Century Foundation. Reprinted by permission from *The Christian Century*.

27. Lamentations 1:12 (RSV).

28. In the course of the three remaining chapters of this study, further attention is given to the problem of ethical motivation and strategy within the framework of Christian faith.

Chapter : SIX

Irony and the Gospel of Group Interest

As implied in the chapter on folk religion, an appraisal
of the piety of group interest does not involve wholly
different considerations from the evaluation of the different points of view we have been since considering.

A Mutual Admiration Society

Folk religion assumes transparent and fully developed
form in the domestication of faith to the interests of the
nation. Illustrations are readily at hand. Norman Vincent
Peale serves as an adviser to the Christian Freedom Foundation. He has published an article in *The Reader's Digest*
on the subject, "Let the Church Speak Up for Capitalism." [1] Billy Graham, who has written that "America is in
deep water and our very survival depends on our moral
and spiritual strength," has addressed the annual conference of International Christian Leadership. But the

119

traffic along the road of sympathy between certain religious interests and the national interest is noticeably two-way. What the "national interest" is taken to mean varies, of course, with the individual and the group. The present national administration has evidently been affected by the new revivalism. Vice President Nixon attended the Yankee Stadium rally of the Graham crusade, affirming in the course of his invited remarks that the most noteworthy thing about Billy Graham is that he "believes." How often have Americans been assured, especially by prominent public figures, that their country's spiritual heritage (whatever that might mean) is their greatest weapon (whatever that too might mean) in the fight against world communism? The citizenry appears firmly united by the bodies that make them all Americans and by the souls that make them realize what a wonderful thing religion is. The supposition that religion ought to be good for the group lies, as we have seen, at the very center of folk religion.

The Nemesis of Patriotic Piety

Now if the socio-political order is indeed instituted of God, lack of proper loyalty to the nation and the secular group is certainly a moral defect. Deficiency in this area can be interpreted as social irresponsibility. The fault is compounded when men fail to make relative ethical judgments between nations and between politico-economic systems. Who can be so indiscriminate as to equate the moral health of world communism with that of Western democracy?

Unlike the cult of reassurance, the gospel of group interest in its nationalist form speaks much of the crisis of our culture. Indeed, its announced intent, as typified in the literature of International Christian Leadership, is to aid in resolving that crisis.

Christianity is proposed as the method of operation. Thus, the men of International Christian Leadership join with others who, out of anxiety for the fate of this nation, turn to the Christian faith for help. The irony is that any spiritual resource which can supposedly supply such aid is always less than Christian faith, since, according to the Christian faith, men cannot count upon God for the resources needed to insure the success of human causes. The weakness men feel forces them to seek strength, but unfortunately the strength of the Christian faith is the weakness that is put to death on a cross. This is why the prudential help that desperate men imagine they receive from the Christian faith is actually conceived in the vain imagination of their hearts. It is, in short, not truth but superstition.

In the context of the issue of irony the important practical and moral question is whether the gospel of group interest furnishes a positive solution to men's problems or whether it merely intensifies their difficulties. Just what do the exponents of that gospel have in mind when they speak of the "welfare" of the nation? It is a fact of great seriousness that in the second half of the twentieth century the problem of national welfare cannot be divorced at all from a compelling, almost unbearable interdependence of the nations. Intrinsic to "piety along the Potomac" and its counterparts across the land is the employment of God as an ally. Is this *really* to promote the common welfare? We live in a time when mutual annihilation by the nations is a dread and constant possibility. The god of the gospel of national interest is assigned the function of exalting the nation. This is self-defeating, for, unfortunately, the net effect of commitment to a national god is that by compounding the rivalries and jealousies of nations and by helping to range people against people, that god only increases the threat of national and mutual destruction.

Matter, Spirit, and Responsibility

Simone de Beauvoir, the French author, has written that the great American hoaxes are based, not on lies, but on virtues ably exploited. The arrogance of the American nation is not a matter of love of power; "it is the love of imposing on others that which is good." Part of this arrogance is related to the American love for transmuting half truths into total truths. A glaring illustration is the condemnation of communism for its materialism. Theoretical communism is undoubtedly materialistic in the sense of assuming, on the one hand, that in the ultimate nature of things, "matter" has priority over "mind" and, on the other hand, that the things that really count in human affairs are essentially economic in character. But the charge of materialism in these respects is hardly a fitting one for Americans to make. Coming as it does from a people possessed of the highest standard of living in the world, surely the charge has fallen bitterly on the ears of the miserable masses of humanity, for whom the materialism practiced by the Communists assumes—wrongly, in an ultimate sense—the form of spiritual deliverance.

It is particularly ironic that so many of those who work at the new piety of condemning Communist materialism in behalf of "Christian spirituality" are among our most prosperous citizens.[2] One of the best ways to turn the uncommitted nations to communism is through this very charge of materialism. Nicolas Berdyaev, himself a great foe of communism, wrote on one occasion, "The question of bread for myself is a material question, but the question of bread for my neighbors, for everybody, is a spiritual and a religious question." Man does not live by bread alone, but without bread he does not live at all. The whole attempt to distinguish the "material" side of life from the "spiritual" side might make some practical sense to Communists, but it ought hardly make sense to Christians. It is foreign to the biblical tradition of the unity of life, a tradition of which Christians are reputedly the heirs.

Time expended in verbal denunciations of the Communists from an allegedly Christian perspective would be spent more profitably in fostering deeds of mercy, responsible and imaginative leadership, and creative counsel to this time of troubles. The critical and continuing need to combine firmness with patience in our international policies for action is not helped at all by compounding American fears of all the godless men in the Kremlin.

Variations on the Theme of Idolatry

The spiritual problem in opposing communism is how to meet its idolatries without falling prey to greater idolatries.[3] In the program of International Christian Leadership there is an implicit idolatry of making Christian faith an adjunct to the struggle against communism. There is also an explicit idolatry. Christian leaders are singled out as somehow the peculiar hope of the world. "Communism and other materialistic ideas find adherents *only when* Christian leadership falters or is absent." Men and women committed to Christ are to be produced for *"key positions* of leadership the world over." [4] Apart from the quandary of exactly how this latter scheme is to be implemented, one is constrained to wonder how familiar the International Christian Leadership people are with the comparative behaviors of non-Christians and of Christians in politics across the years and across the globe. Evidently this group does not know, or does not want to know, of the many avowed secularists who work so responsibly to keep back the menace of communism. Further, the men of International Christian Leadership surely will have heard of the "committed Christian leaders" of South Africa and of America who have held to a remarkably similar piety to that affirmed by this very organization and yet have called upon such piety in order to support racial segregation and discrimination.[5] Presumably, International Christian Leadership would shrink from such discrimination. On the other hand, one can hardly be blamed for wondering what would happen to this group's Christian aspirations were they permitted to adjudicate the earthly fate of a number of Communists.

It is important to note that the strategy advocated by this organization not only agrees with that of such groups as Spiritual Mobilization and the Christian Freedom Foundation but directly parallels that of Billy Graham. Transformed individuals will save the world.[6] Graham's idolatries are less exclusive, however, or, in other terms, more democratic. He does not limit his utopian hopes to leaders; much room is provided for the saving power of converted common men. In any case, International Christian Leadership and Graham are united by an ironic failure to recognize that basic moral strategy, to be effective, must be primarily social and political rather than primarily religious. Religious faith can foster and support ethical incentive and purpose, but zeal for action remains ineffectual until it is wedded to socio-political instrumentalities. Faith is continually tempted, on the one hand, to make itself idolatrous at the ideological level through confusing its cause with God's cause and, on the other hand, to make itself idolatrous at the practical level through imagining that it can somehow directly implement social tasks and international policy.

These considerations immediately raise the question of a common front with those who do not necessarily agree with us religiously. As Will Herberg has pointed out,

It is one thing to say that no real justification for our kind of democracy or real dynamic in its defense against Communist totalitarianism is possible that does not draw upon the insights and resources of Jewish-Christian faith; it is another and vastly different thing to say that only those who explicitly avow this faith can be included in the democratic front against Communism.[7]

The problem of a common front becomes even more serious when a group that could profit from such co-operation restricts itself to "Christian leaders." As a contrast to such restriction, there is another group which, in its first years at least, has avoided the idolatries of International Christian Leadership. The reference is to the Foundation for Religious Action in the Social and Civil Order.[8] The Foundation seeks, according to its statement of aims, "to strengthen the moral and religious foundations of Democracy" and to unite "all believers in God" in the struggle between democracy and communism. The leadership of the Foundation does not wish to turn American democracy into a religious absolute, but it is nevertheless concerned lest fear of the perils of an unexamined piety be permitted to cut the nerve of responsible moral action. This point of view is much more defensible ethically than the effort of International Christian Leadership to make Christianity and the God of Christian faith virtual allies of the nation against communism. In the light of the issue posed by religious restrictions upon personnel within International Christian Leadership, it is significant that the Foundation for Religious Action is organized on an avowedly interfaith basis. A lesson suggested by the contrast between the two groups is that representatives of the Christian faith, through collaboration with men who believe differently, may be saved from some of their own idolatries.

The attempt to subject universal divine truth to particular human purposes has been made for centuries. Our nation is coaxed to join the gruesome parade of many elder brothers and many deceased members of the family of nations. One of the most striking testimonies to the continuing hardness of the human heart is that, no matter how many times men see before their eyes the failure of nationalist cults, they want to initiate new ones. As recently as World War I, Jesus of Nazareth was drafted and fitted out in a U. S. Army uniform. Subsequent penitence for this and similar ventures has been succeeded of late by new covenants between religion and the national advantage. These too must fail.

All in all, America's "turn to religion" gives little evidence of diminishing the nation's self-righteousness in the counsels of the nations. As bearers of a historical and spiritual tradition which regards this country as somehow "innocent" of the warring propensities of nations, and as citizens of one of the two most powerful countries in the world, the temptation is almost overwhelming for Americans to see in their religiosity proof of their virtue. As a people they already have a proclivity for making wooden and moralistic distinctions between the good guys and the bad guys. It is not only idolatrous but ironic when religion puts a stamp of holy approval on a Cowboy-and-Indian mentality. America could do with less of the religion that induces self-righteousness and promotes self-interest and with more of the faith that fosters humility and implements social responsibility, lest vanity turn the nation's strength into weakness and its wisdom into folly.

"Free Enterprise," Human and Divine

Appraisal of the gospel of group interest would be incomplete without consideration of its more explicitly economic forms.

Many men have maintained that the business of religion is to conserve and further social values. Émile Durkheim's well-known theory of the genesis and inspiration of religion among men sought to account for the persistence of religion precisely on the basis of man's reverence for the group. There is no irony in either the claim or the theory as such. The possibility of irony arises when, from the standpoint of one's own ideals, religious faith *ought* to play a more creative role than reconciliation with a given economic procedure and yet may, in point of fact, turn out to do little more than support that practice. Irony draws even closer where one's ideals include the supremacy of the individual over the group but where the application of the ideal may, in fact, lead to the subordination of the individual to a particular ideology. These are among the major perplexities that accompany the religious support of libertarianism in economic and political life.

If the substance of folk piety is religion in alliance with both human interests and human ideals, the spiritual representatives of "free enterprise" concentrate consciously on the latter. They stand for the ideal of individual liberty. Spokesmen for Spiritual Mobilization and for the Christian Freedom Foundation, organizations identified in Chapter Two, could never concede that they comprehend the Christian faith from the perspective of particular economic interests. Such a refusal would not be a matter of dishonesty. Those whom prosperity has favored cannot wholly avoid the logic of their Calvinist forebears that the material blessings of this world are really the blessings of the Lord, bestowed not so much out of grace as out of the merit of honest toil. These Christian libertarians are honestly convinced that their programs apply the Christian faith to the welfare of men. We can hardly criticize them constructively at the point of motivation.

Sincerity of motive does not, unfortunately, preclude idolatry in practice. Thus, *Faith and Freedom,* the journal of Spiritual Mobilization, in assuring its readers that "the Creator's changeless principles" are further discovered and applied through the efforts of the libertarian, has insisted that it does not work for any special interest. Freedom "is in the interest of every man of faith." Such alleged universalism, already restricted by the two words at the end of the phrase just quoted, is further inhibited by the absolute fear that a socialist state is *always* the enemy of the free man and that a democratic government practicing paternalism "straightway becomes such an enemy." *Christian Economics,* organ of the Christian Freedom Foundation, maintains that the "free market" is "the economic system" that contains the "greatest amount of Christianity." Consistent with this doctrine, an ex-congressman has written in the latter publication that an "ethical result" is guaranteed by "the competitive, private property system regardless of the motives of its managers. . . . Yes, 'God works in wondrous ways His marvels to perform.' " [9]

The stumbling block here is that God may have other ideas. As Liston Pope once remarked, if we are ever informed that God's creation of the world was the first application of the principle of free enterprise, we shall have heard everything. It is one thing to advocate economic libertarianism on grounds of rational or empirical argument. Adam Smith may have been proved largely mistaken by subsequent events, but he was no fool. It is quite another matter, however, to conceive God in the image of Adam Smith. Whenever the Christian faith is made absolutely harmonious with a particular socio-economic scheme, that faith is debased. Men come to worship their own ideas and works, not after the fashion of the atheist or humanist, but in the name of God. At this point the avowed secularist is in a morally superior position to the religious man. At least the secularist does not corrupt his own interests by assigning them to the will of a universal God.

"The American Way" and the American Tradition

Judgment upon the idolatries of the economic libertarianism of the spirit is supplemented by more practical criteria of irony.

The spiritual mobilizers speak much of "the American way." How thoroughly do they represent it? They stand for that side of the American tradition which says that religion has an obligation whenever occasion demands to speak out in criticism of the state. But they subscribe to

a highly truncated version of the doctrine that the secular
and social powers have been instituted of God. The mobilizers of the spirit have come to betray that side of the
tradition which holds that the spiritual realm must stand
under social judgment. At this juncture, the folk religion
of these spokesmen is neither strong enough nor consistent
enough. When loyalty to religion goes too far in the direction of individualism, it may be flaunting the divine purpose instead of reflecting it. This may be one reason that
apart from the presence of certain conflicts of economic
interest, the spiritual mobilizers have never succeeded in
mobilizing the masses of the American people. The "common man" has been taught that religion, to be good, must
be good for the people. He also keeps in his heart the
American ideology of libertarian idealism. But he carries
in his bones and in his head the wisdom of practical and
social experience. He knows that when, as often happens,
a house thief is on the prowl, he ought to call the police.
And he knows too that when a railroad is being stolen, the
thing to do is to call the government. The "common man"
has just enough Calvinism left inside to remember that
people who come around and, in the name of the life of
the "spirit," chat friendly-like about the dignity of the
individual, may actually have their eye on his wallet more
than on his soul. (This observation is not a substitute for,
but a supplement of, the realization that the "common
man" finds "social security" highly enjoyable.)

Man the Measure

Criticism of "free enterprise" religion from the standpoint of the Christian faith and criticism from the point
of view of the American tradition are joined in the under-

standing of the nature of man which is to some extent
shared by both the faith and the tradition.

Although the spiritual mobilizers well understand freedom in the sense of the rights of the individual, they know
little of freedom in its total anthropological dimension.
By the latter is meant the human power to transcend whatever is "there," the strange capacity in men to stand in
imagination outside themselves and their world and to
contemplate both.[10]

An ironic aspect of Christian libertarianism in economic
and political life is that it does not actually stand for the
freedom of man that it tries to celebrate. It simply does
not comprehend the freedom of man in all its height and
depth. Through this failure Christian libertarianism is led
to misconstrue the actual relation between freedom and
order in human society. The libertarians fall prey to the
illusion that social order must follow as the automatic
consequence of the assertion of human individuality.
Though, from one point of view, this position maintains
"high" expectations of the consequences of human behavior, it has, from another point of view, too "low" an
estimate of man. The power of transcendence may, to be
sure, issue in the sort of righteous activity that serves the
community. But the equally live alternative is that individuals will make themselves and their interests the final
center of reference for their thinking and behavior within
the society in which they move. To know oneself as a
self is, alas, to serve the self, even at the expense of others.
Here enters the inevitable and explosive eventuality that
human freedom will undermine social order rather than
advance human rights. In this way individual liberty and
dignity are themselves put in jeopardy. This is where so-

cial constraint becomes a necessity, not so much because man is "selfish" as because his freedom knows no limits.

Christian libertarians and Christian nonlibertarians alike will agree that "limited government" in the American tradition means that the state cannot be permitted to have too much power. Both sides are foes of tyranny. But the former group advocates a government that is limited to the promotion of the libertarian cause. The latter group holds, by contrast, that the government and various other social instrumentalities must also act to set limits upon the behavior of men, not in the name of arbitrary control but in the name of the very freedom that is the distinctive mark of man. This latter point of view realizes the wisdom of the "founding fathers" in establishing a political system of checks and balances. These men possessed practical insight into the paradoxical truth that on the one hand, the individual has received certain inalienable rights from his Creator and that on the other hand, no individual or group is good enough to have wide control over men. The spiritual mobilizers are zealous to insist upon both these things but they restrict the second point to a philosophy for government only, and they fail to see that the insight is equally relevant to the possession and application of economic power.

For earlier libertarian followers of Adam Smith an "unseen hand" moved within the shadows, guiding the free economic process to "serve the commonweal" through each man "seeking his own." Unfortunately, the "unseen hand" is more than unseen; it is nonexistent. Unrestrained men quickly fill the vacuum that remains through acts that threaten, rather than serve, the commonweal. Acknowledgment of this situation is a bond between the tradition of American democracy and the understanding of man in the Christian faith.[11] The only "unseen hand" that Christian faith recognizes is the hand of the Lord who stands in judgment upon all of men's economic and political arrangements.

In sum, the irony in spiritual mobilization for "free enterprise" is a particularly serious form of irony because it has secular as well as theological dimensions: (1) The strength in the underwriting of "free enterprise" becomes weakness through the vanity of its association with "the Creator's changeless principles." There is a certain grotesqueness in maintaining that "free enterprise" is modern man's implementation of the spiritual freedom that the New Testament proclaims. The freedom of the New Testament actually offers men a vantage point from which to judge and find wanting any and every economic system, including that of *laissez-faire* capitalism, and any and every "spiritual" enterprise, including that which seeks to mobilize men for the promotion of economic libertarianism. (2) The virtue of appealing to "the American way" becomes vice through a sin of omission. In the American tradition in its totality the life of the spirit is subject to social and moral judgment just as much as the secular realm is subject to religious judgment. (3) The wisdom of the mobilizers of the spirit is not great enough to avoid folly. In failing to allow for the full freedom of man, they prove themselves to be not the ally but the foe of human freedom in its full dimension.

Implicit in the analysis within this and the two preceding chapters is the question of social conformism as a possible causative influence upon contemporary American religious life. This question requires specific consideration.

Notes

1. See Miller, "The Gospel of Norman Vincent Peale," *op. cit.*, p. 21.
2. It is often pointed out that a great deal of the support of the recent religious revival, and particularly the financial support, comes from men who represent extremely conservative socio-economic policies and interests.
3. Will Herberg, "Communism, Democracy, and the Churches," *Commentary,* Apr. 1955, p. 392.
4. Italics added in both quotations.
5. Many Christian leaders in South Africa and this country have, of course, strongly opposed this behavior.
6. We do not mean to give the impression that these groups exert massive influence upon American life. The notion that the answer to the problems and conflicts of social and international life rests uniquely in the efforts of men distinguished by their moral and spiritual character is, nevertheless, deeply ingrained in the attitudes of Americans.
7. Herberg, *op. cit.*, p. 393.
8. This organization has headquarters in Washington, D. C. Its chairman and executive director is Charles W. Lowry.
9. Samuel B. Pettingill, "Only the Free Can Be Strong," *Christian Economics,* Apr. 10, 1951, as quoted in John A. Hutchison, ed., *Christian Faith and Social Action* (New York: Charles Scribner's Sons, 1953), p. 25.
10. This paragraph and the two that follow reproduce in altered form passages from an article of the writer, "The Christian and Secular Answer to the Dilemma of Freedom and Order," *Christianity and Crisis,* Dec. 28, 1953, pp. 172-175.
11. Those who have sought to make Socialism *the* Christian politico-economic system face the same practical difficulty as the spiritual mobilizers, but from the opposite side. The question of how individuals may be restrained becomes one of who will plan the planners. The answer is that unless the system as a whole is subject to continuing checks and balances and to free democratic processes, social order will outrun individual freedom. "Eternal vigilance is the price of liberty."

Chapter : SEVEN

Irony, Conformity, and Conformism

The strong element of sincerity in the new American religion renders more difficult an already baffling question: Is the surge of piety, within as well as without the churches, a matter of conformism in the guise of religion? Representatives of American popular piety could scarcely be expected to answer yes. To ignore their convictions is hardly an objective approach. However, to fail to go beyond such testimony is equally deficient from the standpoint of objectivity.

Conformist Temptations

Is it not the case that, generally speaking, American society as a whole has turned markedly in a conformist direction? To the extent that this is so, it would be surprising if religion were not subjected in a substantial way to conformist influences. Seldom, if ever, does religion remain free of social conditioning.

135

The question of whether the turn to piety is to be interpreted as an embodiment of conformism turns, in consequence, upon two specific procedures: (1) The upsurge in religion ought to be related seriously to relevant understanding of the state of American society. (2) Inquiry must be made whether there is independent evidence of predominantly conformist tendencies in the new piety. That these two questions are finally inseparable is seen in the fact that the problem of conformism in religion is, in the nature of the case, fundamentally a social problem. It is not possible to supply here final answers to either of these problems. The material that follows may, however, be of some aid to further needed reflection.

One ground for caution in listening to lamentations over the surrender of the individual to the crowd is that these are formulated largely by a minority of relatively individualistic intellectuals. Perhaps this limited representation is inevitable because intellectuals tend to monopolize the conversation on such matters. At the risk of incurring the guilt of association with the anti-intellectuality of much of American life, we must, nevertheless, ask: What is the guarantee that our sophisticated social critics possess uniquely authoritative insight into the state of modern man's soul? [1]

The most concrete extreme from reliance upon these men—who, of course, are not at all of one pessimistic mind —is the use of public opinion techniques. Do people conceive themselves to be as dehumanized as some of the "eggheads" insist? Regrettably, this opposite approach hardly settles the matter satisfactorily. A judgment frequently brought against the methodology of "tests and measurements" is that devices such as questionnaires are hardly able to ferret out the inner decisions and dispositions of men.

To give the more cynical intellectuals their due for a moment, it is theoretically quite possible that people have reached the sorry state of no longer being *aware* that they are as sheep with too many shepherds. In speaking of "the eclipse of man in modern industrial work," Douglas V. Steere makes reference to

> well-paid voices of the industrial order who, upon the basis of elaborate polling, declare unanimously that man cannot be eclipsed by the present order because these surveys show that this order is giving him just what he wants. These bold voices of the future go on to show that when questioned, the industrial worker insists that he *likes* monotony, that he *enjoys* the almost complete irresponsibility of modern industrial work, and that he would not for anything in the world live anywhere else than in a vast industrial city. Far from repudiating the shading out of man in the present industrial system, such testimonies, which have been so painstakingly and accurately gathered and reported, may only go to show how far the disease has advanced, how much of the eclipse has already taken place.[2]

Unfortunately, all this does not help very much here. Apparently, modern industrial man does not look upon himself as lost, but supposedly the "egghead," who is not himself wholly lost since he knows all about lostness, has succeeded in discerning the plight of the common man, a plight of which the latter is not aware. So there we are.

If attention to inner attitudes fails to get us very far, the obvious alternative is to concentrate on overt behavior. This appears to establish firmer, more objective footing. Yet, this approach does not resolve the real dilemma. The assigning of priority to external evidence over inner states of mind is not self-justifying. It is, in the last resort, an arbitrary choice.

Further, even at the level of objective evidence, the analyst must be extremely wary of equating conformity with conformism. There is no necessary evil in conformity. Many men speak approvingly of conformity to the truth and conformity to the will of God, of conformity to the law and conformity in the sense of serious action to meet the legitimate needs of others. It is not until acts of conformity are infected by slavishness that conformism obtains. When men testify to the truth only under compulsion and when they observe a divine command only under fear of punishment, when people obey traffic ordinances only under the eye of an agent of society and when they meet their brothers' needs only through fear of social censure—under these conditions the disease of conformism has set in. Conforming thoughts and deeds are preserved from conformism by free, responsible decision. A man may purchase a ranch house because he lacks the gumption to stand out from the crowd, but then too he may do it because he honestly believes that this style of living furthers the welfare of his family. It would be difficult for him to choose a ranch house unless there were such things. And it may well have been social pressure that started him thinking about a ranch house in the first place. These are points where social constraint enters. Yet, it hardly follows that the buyer of a ranch house does not make a responsible choice.

We Organization Men

Must we insist that in contemporary American life the only decisive stimulus to acts of conformity is slavish conformism? As a means of exploring this question further, we refer to a widely quoted study by William H. Whyte, Jr., entitled *The Organization Man.* [3] Whyte represents, of course, the broad class of intellectuals whose wisdom we have in some measure questioned. A redeeming aspect of his attitude and work is that he avoids the prejudice of reducing people to slaves of "the system."

Whyte cannot be accused of underestimating the pervasive power of conformist trends. The thesis of *The Organization Man* is that as a nation America has been undergoing a subtle and basic shift from an individualistic ethic to a social ethic. By the latter term Whyte means "the contemporary body of thought which makes morally legitimate the pressures of society against the individual." The group becomes the source of creativity; the individual's worth is estimated on the basis of his collaboration with others.

Americans continue to pride themselves on their adherence to an individualistic ethic and they tell themselves that they still practice it. Any eulogy for the American Dream is a virtual definition of the ethic of individualism, a standard Americans continue officially to hold. As Whyte puts it, "Whatever the embroidery, there is almost always the thought that pursuit of individual salvation through hard work, thrift, and competitive struggle is the heart of the American achievement."

The sober truth is that the harsh facts of organization society have come to stand in conflict with this ethic—a development which, if Whyte is correct in this judgment, seriously dates a number of Norman Vincent Peale's steps for staying alive all one's life. Is Horatio Alger now dead? If so, then Peale, Spiritual Mobilization, and the Christian Freedom Foundation join the few surviving older top men in the corporations in not being able to bring themselves to bury the corpse.[4]

Whyte is not beguiled into a blanket indictment of modern "mass society" as such. Some, in oversimple fashion, have made this charge.[5] The decisive issue is whether the social ethic is to be identified with conformism. Whyte does not think so. There is another, more hopeful side to the story. It is grounded in the genuine moral elements that are a constituent part of the social ethic. Every individual faces the painful moral dilemma of ascertaining *when* he has surrendered to the group. Whyte makes an important distinction between conformity and unwitting conformity. Unwitting conformity may entail conformism (as we have defined the latter term), but witting conformity transcends pure conformism. Many of the suburbanites Whyte talks so much about are remarkably knowledgeable concerning their "plight." The person who is possessed of some insight into the actions of himself and his group is by virtue of that very fact not wholly imprisoned in impersonal pressures.

As Whyte says, it is not despite the success of their group life that suburbanites "are troubled but partly because of it, for that much more do they feel an obligation to yield to the group." There is really no final answer to this dilemma, although recognition of it helps. The more benevolent the group, the more one must be on guard against it. Nevertheless, there remains the sure conviction, however obscured by fears, that response to the demands and needs of people is a moral responsibility. Whyte offers the conclusion that the foundation of the social ethic is not conformity (conformism in our usage) but "a sense of moral imperative." In the light of his previous emphases upon the social pressures that threaten to submerge the individual, this conclusion seems rather too generous. Whyte is wrestling here with the age-old and thorny issue of human freedom and fatefulness and, generally speaking, one can ask from him no more consistency than the two dimensions within that enigma make possible.

Perhaps the primary value of Whyte's study is that in so many words, he declines to offer a *solution*. This sounds un-American but he has the courage to refuse to answer. "There is no solution. The conflict between individual and society has always involved dilemma; it always will, and it is intellectual arrogance to think a program would solve it." Yet, so long as the conflict goes on, there is reason to take heart. Every time a man says no, he strikes at the Achilles' heel of conformism.[6]

We have not sought to prove here, by the easy (and conformist) device of quoting from another book, that conformity is not conformism. To talk about the organization man and suburbia is not to talk about all America. However, it would appear that much in contemporary American life is actually epitomized in this way. In so far as it is justifiable to hold that, *of all places,* the structure of our organizational life is not necessarily ridden with conformism, there is some cause for doubt that conformism has come to rule American society as a whole. Precisely because Whyte is so thoroughly aware of, and concerned over, the pervasiveness of the new groupism, it is our belief that due attention ought to be given to such evidences of freedom and responsibility as, according to him, continue to persist. Whyte does document his thesis in impressive ways which we cannot take the space to reproduce.[7] He is saying, from the standpoint of sophisticated social criticism, what the traditional Christian understanding of man has long affirmed in two of its facets: First, no matter what happens to men in the world, they possess a residual freedom as children of God. The slave camps and the brainwashings have brought this home. Men may always say no, even if the result is torture and even death. Second, obligation to others is a genuine value. The individual always faces the responsibility of deciding for himself what he owes to himself and what he owes to the group. The new groupism itself contains an important truth about man, something that is twisted into a half-truth only when it is made the whole truth. We refer to the recognition, however unconscious, that human beings are made for life in community. "God setteth the solitary in families." [8]

These tentative judgments seem justified: We live in a time when the relatively elastic conformities of normally ordered life have undeniably been subjected to pressures leading to social conformism. In the America of the second half of the twentieth century the social signals are set at "Caution." As the author of *The Organization Man* himself agrees, the dominant strain in popular culture is apparently adjustment to the system. To presume that conformist tendencies simply mean conformity in the good sense is to ignore ever-menacing threats to freedom. The tremendous accent upon the value of adjustment in American culture can aid people as ends in themselves only within highly restricted limits. It can also mold them to the dominant social structure. Nevertheless, to interpret conformity as nothing but conformism is to fail to consider both the supports of human individuality that permeate the American tradition and also the power of that residual human freedom which stubbornly persists in every social situation.

To pursue further the issue of the degree of conformism

within the body social would be to stray too far from the
bounds of this study. What may we say of the more specifically relevant issue of conformist elements in the surge
of American piety?

Conformism and the New Piety

Speaking of the continuing religious situation in twentieth-century America, Herbert W. Schneider associates
majority elements in American religion with general social complacency and an ignorance of the sweeping and
revolutionary changes that have occurred in the human
world. "This unimaginative, complacent population, which
can accept the changes since 1900 as merely external
and superficial comprises the central core of the American
people and accounts for more than half of its religious
practices and ideas." [9] On this view, it is not conformism
in any positive or conscious sense but conformism by de-
fault that pervades the religious life. The people are half
asleep.

The Christian Century has gone further than this. A
recent editorial suggests that part of the moral and spiritual complacency of Americans is "probably a tightly
clutched camouflage, hiding driving fears beneath a
pseudo-serenity." [10] The anxieties of the people keep them
from sleeping soundly. The 1957 Billy Graham revival in
New York City has served as the occasion for *The Christian Century* to deplore the contrived mass religion of our
time. An irony of the Graham crusade was that even
though its leaders prayed for success, a certain kind of
success was antecedently guaranteed.

. . . Operating in a period of enormous popular religious interest, anything this obviously religious is bound to compel the

multitudes. The prearranged crowds, though they guarantee the "success," are only part of the story. In a time of bewilderingly generalized and undifferentiated and uncritical religious interest, it is certain that the standees and turn-away throngs will be there for their own reasons, too. Here is something hugely religious and everybody is religious like everybody else, so why not go to the Garden? They all read Norman Vincent Peale and they all watch Bishop Sheen and they all go to the big Easter showing of *The Ten Commandments* and they all believe in records like "I Believe," so why not go to the Garden?

. . . The most worrisome aspect of the whole Graham phenomenon, perhaps, has been the failure of nerve in men who know better, the atrophy of critical faculties, the bandwagon scramble, the soporific requirements of good will. Worst of all has been the drive to smother opposition, to engulf critics, to surround criticism. In the good name of unity, Billy Graham and his friends have pressed for a dangerously anti-Protestant uniformity and conformity. We would count ourselves among those who have resisted that, and are resisting that, and shall resist that. . . .[11]

There is much sober truth here, although it does seem that *The Christian Century* overstates its case (something that almost seems compellingly necessary in truly prophetic judgments).

The preceding analysis of William H. Whyte, Jr.'s study has implications for the more immediate problem of conformism and the turn to religion. Do adherents of the new piety conform automatically, or do they also make autonomous decisions? Have they been subjected only to external compulsions, or is it also out of genuine responsibility, obligation, and conviction that they believe and act as they do? To assert that all-or-nothing points of view are suspect is to utter a truism, but one that is not always long remembered. We submit that those who reduce our surge of piety to mere conformism (as, of course, *The Christian Century* does not) and those (if there are such) who discern within that piety no conformist strains at all are both wrong. This criticism applies particularly when attention is directed to piety at the group level, but the two elements just mentioned are no doubt present in many individuals.

A needed attitude of caution toward alleged values in the new religion ought not derive simply from concern over the fact that "everybody is doing it." A wiser approach—although an infinitely more puzzling one—lies in ascertaining where and when conformity entails conformism and then trying hard to apply this experience to specific groups and individuals. From what was said at the beginning of this chapter respecting the elusiveness of motivation, it is not possible to calculate in any exact or conclusive way that conformist dispositions are gaining a final victory today. Perhaps this puts us in the position of recommending the impossible. To advocate a metrical technique for assessing the new piety would be to fall into a frame of mind itself conditioned by mass thinking and the new groupism. Nevertheless, one is not forced into silence. From such external evidence as is available, there is little doubt that social conformism occupies a formidable place in the new piety. In so far as individual responsibility is considered a general good, it follows that the stronger the trend to conformism in religion the firmer is the obligation to react critically to that trend.

One saving paradox is that although the incentive to religious faith often derives from social pressure, the subsequent effect of faith upon people may be to lift them significantly beyond conformism. Doors are opened to

fresh and challenging perspectives. Faith may break free
from its dubious origins, now deriving its dynamic from
independent conviction and perchance even from the
Holy Spirit.

A contrasting paradox brings us back to the problem
of ironic strains in the new piety. Since religion in the
American tradition does not merely conserve the social
mores and folkways but is also supposed to provide men
an independent vantage point for judging all of life, we
presume that many religious men, including a number
of agnostics who are sympathetic to religion, hold in common that religion ought to be an emancipating force. To
the extent that the new piety does not liberate, but only
intensifies the conformism that has already fastened itself
upon people, irony takes command. In the very act of
searching, if half consciously, for an escape from their
aloneness, the men of the days of big religion may only
find themselves trampled underfoot by the lonely crowd.

Enter the Church

To conform to the crowd is to violate one's own freedom; to flee from the crowd is to invite loneliness. Is there
anywhere a "crowd" that is more than a crowd, an "organization" that is more than an organization? To ask
this is to raise the issue of the role of the Christian Church.
We have been taught that the churches have been assigned
responsibility for the care and cure of souls. Will the
churches uphold men in their freedom as sons of God,
as meanwhile human loneliness is purged through the
blessed community?

A number of people who have shown sympathy for the
new American piety, particularly in its "peace of mind"

and revivalist forms, insist that the new religion would never have gained such success were it not for the failure of the churches. Many who speak in this way are themselves committed churchmen. From the perspective of the present study, there is neither moral nor Christian justification for a blind defense of the churches. Much of the criticism indicated is well taken. The churches have failed and will doubtless continue to fail.

However, it is neither fair nor Christian to neglect the other side of the matter. At least two factors are relevant. For one thing, the churches are made up of human beings who are themselves subject to the limitations and temptations of all men. Thus, we must speak of the Church as the Body of Christ rather than as Christ himself or even as the embodiment of the Spirit of Christ. The symbol of "body" points to the finite condition of the Church in this world. The only way that the "superiority" of devout Christians can be defended is through their humble admission of "inferiority," an admission which can be itself used, of course, as an instrument of aggrandizement. George A. Buttrick has stated that the best answer to the charge of so many hypocrites in the churches is that "there is always room for one more." The human constituency of the true Church is composed not of perfect men but of forgiven sinners. The Church in its ideal form witnesses not to the achievements of men but to the free grace of God in Jesus Christ.

Second, and by similar reasoning, when people turn away from the churches, it may be as much their offense as that of the churches. The Christian church is custodian of a faith which cannot adjust itself to purely human preferences and demands. When men seek to refashion the Church after their own image, the Christian gospel insists that they must inevitably be disappointed.

Can men, nevertheless, count upon the Body of Christ to reveal the good ways that are often hidden to the social view? In its continuing struggle against a divisive individualism, the Christian community runs the risk of losing sight of the individual. The churches are confronted today with the hard task of maintaining their independence of the "other-directed" conformisms of suburbia and its counterparts. A complication is that within the churches of recent years much value has been placed upon social adjustment and simple harmonies among men. The Christian community is now charged with a great work of re-education, whereby these partial goods can be placed in a much wider moral framework. The churches must make plain that adjustment and reconciliation can only be to God rather than to any *status quo*, including a supposedly divine one.[12] Moreover,

the church is never more surely preparing the way for its own future discomfiture than when it succumbs to the temptation to attract a following by evading the dark facts of human failure and frustration and the ruthlessness of society. . . . There, in an implacably and impersonally immoral society, is where men are caught, and in their efforts to adjust their own good intentions to the conditions of their existence they fall into despair.[13]

The Christian churches are encountering many such strong temptations and many such pressing responsibilities. Happily, whenever these temptations are resisted and these responsibilities fulfilled, every man is helped. To the degree that men today are irresponsibly acquiescent, the Christian community is called to raise the banner of nonconformism—with reference not simply to the new piety but to any and all areas where conformism is a threat. This in no way means that social orneriness is an independent value. The nonconformist conscience is often grossly self-centered. We are not implying that Christian policy is to be devised by the statistical technique of finding out what most people are doing and then standing for the opposite. A Christian perspective ought to be, by contrast, a rational one. Men are warned by the New Testament not to be conformed to the world. This warning introduces the disturbing thought that the role of a Christian in the midst of a prevailingly "religious" climate may be in some situations an "antireligious" one. It was not accidental that in the days of imperial Rome the Christians were called atheists. The label had its own peculiar appropriateness then and it may have it again. The social gods seek hard to reign. The world tempts men with its idolatries. The trouble is that idolatry is not ultimately good for human beings. The Christian church affirms that free human creativity is a real value. This is not humanism in its man-centered version. When human individuality is made into an absolute value, idolatry has simply changed its clothes. We speak rather of men realizing the image of God in which they are made. In other words, the Christian aversion to conformism is theologically based.

Irony is distinguished from pathos and tragedy, says Reinhold Niebuhr, by the fact that ironic situations dissolve when the men responsible become conscious of their complicity in these situations. We have referred to the two possible consequences of this consciousness—either contrition or a desperate growth in vanity that issues in pure evil. If it is true that ironic strains are prevalent in our upsurge of piety, it seems rather doubtful that the promoters of the new religion are going to become conscious of their complicity. Present forms of the new piety will probably go their merry way for a little while, until unforeseen circumstances do something about it. Washington will have more tasty and prayerlike breakfasts. Tin Pan Alley will serenade the people with more hallowed tunes. Norman Vincent Peale will write more best-sellers. Billy Graham's revivals will move from strength to some kind of strength. The mobilizers of the spirit will summon the citizenry to liberty and *laissez faire,* though not to equality or fraternity. And social conformism as a force within the institutions of American religious life will direct the people toward other-directed, successful goals. All this is the American way. We go onward and upward. In this country, the angel charged with the death of the gods always seems so late in arriving. The one comfort is that it finally looks in at every window—quietly but in an inexorable way, dreadfully but with healing in its wings. As Sören Kierkegaard once observed, how consoling is the thought that before the living God everyone is in the wrong.

The allusion above to the place of the Church has already pointed to the need for a positive statement of Christian conviction in the presence of the "turn to religion" in America. To that statement we must turn in a closing chapter.

Notes

1. That the Christian faith of the earliest centuries was carried forward by slaves and common people much more than by intellectuals illustrates the fact that the latter group is not always distinguished for being in close association with decisive social movements.

2. Douglas V. Steere, *Work and Contemplation* (New York: Harper & Brothers, 1957), p. 59. By permission of Harper & Brothers.

3. William H. Whyte, Jr., *The Organization Man* (New York: Simon and Schuster, Inc., 1956). The quotations that follow are included by permission of Simon and Schuster, Inc.

4. This does not imply that the new ethic consciously ranges itself against the individual; on the contrary, its exponents are persuaded that it will help, rather than harm, him. As Whyte puts it, "When a young man says that to make a living these days you must do what somebody else wants you to do, he states it not only as a fact of life that must be accepted but as an inherently good proposition. If the American Dream deprecates this for him, it is the American Dream that is going to have to give. . . ."

5. Compare, for example, Douglas V. Steere's denunciation of mass culture in Chapter Three, *Work and Contemplation* (*op. cit.*).

Any analyst who speaks from an acknowledged Christian standpoint and who then goes on to find that our "mass society" is rotten to the core—as Steere does not—would do well to have his theology inspected. In the Christian view, God is not only Judge but also Creator and Redeemer. To assert that no health at all remains in secular society is to flirt with the heresy that our world has ceased to be God's world.

6. This point is paralleled in a recent observation by a college senior: "Conformity is the name most often given us. Statistics are cited to prove that we are marrying earlier than our predecessors, that we are less adventurous than our forebears, that we are more willing to accept secure jobs and settle down in the cool suburbs than we ought to be. The statistics are probably true. But the fact that we recognize them as true, and are becoming increasingly sensitive to their consequences in our lives, promises that many of us are going to escape the predictions set for our futures. We talk about conformity more than anyone else in history; we read and write books on the subject. As a result of all this talk, increasingly large numbers of us are taking measures to protect ourselves from it." This is from a *Life* article (Feb. 17, 1958, p. 130) which reproduces material from *The Unsilent Gen-*

eration, edited by Otto Butz (New York: Rinehart & Company, Inc., 1958). By permission of Rinehart & Company, Inc.

7. For a sympathetic yet critical commentary on the Whyte volume, see William Lee Miller, "The Organization and the Individual," *Christianity and Crisis,* June 24, 1957. Miller's fundamental objection is that Whyte overemphasizes groupism versus individualism as the key to our problem when the more basic conflict is between human life in depth versus shallowness and triviality. Miller asserts that the latter issue cuts across the other one.

8. Psalms 68:6.

9. Schneider, *Religion in 20th Century America, op. cit.,* p. 13.

10. Editorial, "Tillich on Revivalism," *The Christian Century,* May 8, 1957, p. 582.

11. Editorial, "In the Garden," *The Christian Century, op. cit.* Copyright 1957, Christian Century Foundation. Reprinted by permission from *The Christian Century.* (See also the editorial "Mass Conversions," May 29, 1957).

12. Editorial, "Tillich on Revivalism," *The Christian Century, op. cit.,* pp. 582-583.

13. Paul Hutchinson, "Have We a 'New' Religion?", *Life,* April 11, 1955, p. 158. By permission of Agnes M. Hutchinson, copyright owner.

Chapter : EIGHT

In Search of a Christian Stand

It is so utterly American to live and move and have our being amidst the quantitative bigness of the moment that we are hard put to stand far enough off from ourselves to know exactly what we are doing. The big things become the things that ought to be talked about. Our evaluative energies are consumed in the wrath of whatever dazzles the most. One consequence for the individual who writes books, particularly books about contemporary affairs, is that little else seems to count as long as what he says is "timely," "up to the minute," and "directed to significant trends of the day"—reputedly helping to prove that he has really "put his finger on the pulse" of something or other. The interpreter may come to feel that unless he concentrates on people and events that secure the headlines, he is not working significantly or meaningfully. He may also fall for the illusion that what he says is something long-term and enduring. Confrontation by the sights that dazzle induces this kind of blindness.

Wheels Within Wheels

In actuality, ten or twenty years from now the new American piety may be as dead as the newspapers that reported it. It is rather hard to see how we can stand for very long the terrific pace our surging piety has set for itself. There will probably be a reaction. If the new piety does expire, as it may already have begun to do, the few younger souls who tomorrow or the next day chance to pick up this particular volume will be extremely puzzled over what all the fuss was about. One consolation for us is that the subject matter that has been stressed here—such stuff as headlines are made on—may bear testimony to certain of the relations between religion and society at a particular stage in American history, relations which manifest a strong element of continuity with the past.

Each of us must, in any event, do his level best to maintain a proper sense of historical perspective upon the passing scene in all its transitoriness. More important, we are here concerned with the search for a Christian stand which, in directing a critical word to the religious tendencies under present discussion, may contribute a little to responsible Christian living in these and other days.

It is very difficult for the contemporary American to achieve such a Christian stand. Americans have a strong taboo against finding fault with religion. Though some animosity between religious groups continues to persist, the taboo mentioned applies to behavior toward groups other than one's own. Probably part of the basis for this situation, apart from deficiency in the will to think, is the widespread notion that religion is a personal and private affair. Accordingly, to criticize religion is somehow in bad taste. This applies at the social level as well, for the conviction is also widespread, as we have seen, that religion is a good thing for the community and the nation. Further, for Americans as for many other people, religion retains an inevitable association with holy things. To criticize it seems almost blasphemous. All in all, to disapprove of religion in this country is like being against marriage or education or honest work or perhaps even God himself.

Nevertheless, all of us, soon or late, must come face to face with the issue of personal integrity. Unthinking or silent acceptance of any individual or social standard or form of behavior may imply a shirking of duty within the only historical and cultural situation each of us will ever know.

When we consider what has been happening to some aspects of religion in America, it is not easy to preserve our peace of mind. And yet, we have to grant the probability that not a great deal can be done at the present time to counteract the influence of folk piety. Consider this sobering passage from an article by Will Herberg:

. . . What can the other-directed man or woman [of our society] make of the prophets and the prophetic faith of the Bible? The very notion of being "singled out," of standing "over against" the world, is deeply repugnant to one for whom well being means conformity and adjustment. Religion is valued as conferring a sense of sociability and belonging, a sense of being really and truly *of* the world and society; how can the other-directed man then help but feel acutely uncomfortable with a kind of religion—for that is what biblical faith is—which is a declaration of permanent resistance to the heteronomous claims of society, community, culture, and cult? The other-directed man protects himself against this profoundly disturbing aspect of biblical faith by refusing to understand it; indeed, insofar as he is other-directed, he really *cannot* understand it. The religion he avows is still formally the Jewish or Christian faith rooted in the prophetic tradition; it is, however, so transformed as it passes through the prism of the other-directed mind that it emerges as something quite different, in many ways, its opposite. . . .

. . . The word of faith could be proclaimed and made to thrive in a hostile world, but how can it be communicated in a culture that is all for it but simply will not, cannot, understand it? [1]

Is there, then, no hope? We may continue to look in two directions. Herberg goes on to conclude:

. . . Perhaps after all it is never really possible for man as man, in view of his human dimension of freedom, to reduce himself to an other-directedness that is complete and irretrievable. Perhaps too the hidden power of the divine word, which can shatter the inner-directed man in his pride and self-sufficiency, possesses resources, hitherto unsuspected, enabling it to elude the protective devices of other-direction and to penetrate to the heart of man, whatever his character structure, in his perennial human need for faith and redemption. [2]

Physician, Judge Thyself

As one sets about the task of synoptic evaluation of the surge of American piety, it takes hardly any conscious energy for him to fool himself concerning his true purposes.

Much of the disapproval many in the clergy voice against the leaders of the new piety is probably sour grapes and jealousy. Why could I not have been a Norman Vincent Peale or a Billy Graham? Imagine being called by *Time* Magazine, as Billy Graham has been, "the evan-

gelist of the mid-century"! Why could I not have gained
the hearing and the influence these other men have
achieved? [3]

Much of the opposition to the surge of piety from those
who wish to be identified as intellectuals is probably an
echo from within the emptiness of their own hearts. It is
hard to admit that the world does not know God through
wisdom.[4]

Much of the skepticism and disapprobation that many
have felt simply as individual human beings is probably
due to self-centeredness and a stiff-necked fear of embark-
ing on the venture of faith.

Much of the criticism many voice as occupants of any
one or two or all three of the roles above is probably a
subtle method of trying to raise the level of esteem they
desire third parties to have for them. If they can succeed
in dethroning very important people, they will, by contrast, become that much more important in the eyes of
their audience.

Or will they?

Wholesale castigation of the current American piety
can become simply a new version of the old lament, re-
peated *ad nauseam,* "Look at all the hypocrites in the
churches." The Pharisee lives again to mock all the pub-
licans. The word of the New Testament is ignored, "You
have no excuse, O man, whoever you are, when you judge
another; for in passing judgment upon him you condemn
yourself, because you, the judge, are doing the very same
things." [5]

The only Christian basis on which a man is permitted
to find fault with other people—and it is an answer that
holds only in principle rather than as a release from all
personal anguish—lies in his readiness to be subjected to

the same judgment and to the same standards of morality and faith that he applies to his fellows.

Perhaps all of us, if our plight became desperate enough, would descend to the very forms of religion we criticize as comfortable observers.

The Ways That Are Not Our Ways

Additional reason for hesitation in making adverse judgments lies in the human inability to fathom the methods of God. The prophet Isaiah testifies, "For my thoughts are not your thoughts, neither are your ways my ways, says the Lord." [6] And the Psalmist affirms, "Surely the wrath of men shall praise thee." [7] The Bible as a whole attests that God may use any work of men, as he may use any facet of the total creation, to praise him.

When such words are taken seriously and from the point of view of biblical faith, it is impossible to assert categorically that the surge of piety in America is of no worth at all. As a matter of fact, some churchmen see cause for optimism in what is for them a crucial consideration. May we not anticipate that a revival of religion will contribute to a renewal of faith in God? One clergyman goes so far as to protest,

What is wrong, pray, with religion becoming a vogue in American life? . . . Let's be glad for the faithful fifties.

If this generation will move with the winds of God as we now see them stirring in our American life, we may see one of the most memorable acts of God in the history of mankind. . . .[8]

On this view, the many recent signs of religious interest are to be welcomed, since they may be harbingers of a coming day of victory for the Christian gospel. God may be using the upsurge in religion for his own purposes.

No one can very well deny that there is a certain seeking for God in these popular forms of religion. The admission that God's purposes transcend human knowledge means that the new piety is not to be condemned out of hand. And yet, the words from Isaiah quoted above cut more than one way. Criticism appears justified whenever proponents of the new piety identify their points of view with the will of God or claim a virtual monopoly of insight into the ways of God. Further, who can assert categorically that the turn to piety furnishes any warranty that faith in the living God is growing? And when attention is turned from the issue of our own faith to that of God as our helper, similar reservations are necessary. To the confidence that God will provide peace of mind and help us to "adjust," to the certainty that God must move men at a revival meeting, to the conviction that God is on the side of America or of "Christian economics," and to the assumption that our religious life reflects praiseworthy conformity rather than blameworthy conformism—to all these expectations, one summary answer is quite plausible: The Lord may have different plans.

Because God may be using the surge of piety to further his own sovereign will—what works of men are not utilized in that way?—it does not follow that these forms of piety merit unreserved support. In honest reverence, it may be said that God has his problems and we have ours. The faith that God uses the works of men to praise him is not a measuring tool for making specific human decisions. The absurdity in such an assumption is seen in the fact that one can assert with the same legitimacy that God uses criticisms of the new piety for his divine purposes.

Just what is the point, then, in referring to Isaiah and
to the Psalmist at all? Awareness that in ways beyond un
derstanding, God turns human actions to his own account
implies, first, that God is in every human situation. We
do not have exact knowledge of precisely what God is
about, but we may have the faith that he is at work in
the world. "If I seek thee in religion, thou art already
there! If I seek to escape thee by means of religion, thou
art there!" Second, this awareness implies that in making
critical judgments we are forbidden to play God. No one
has private access to the top secrets of the Most High. In
this respect, blanket or tacit approval of the new piety is
no different in kind from wholesale condemnation. Nei
ther is justified.

The Truth That May Find Us

From the foregoing, it almost seems that we must come
out with little more than mutual denials of the ultimate
validity of each other's point of view. Such negative think
ing is not only untrue to the spirit of Norman Vincent
Peale; it is not a Christian position at all. Christian faith
is never content to stop with the assertion that God's ways
are not our ways.

Are affirmations concerning the ways of God with men
limited to purely human insight? Or do they somehow
rest in divine revelation? If the former is wholly true, any
reaction to the recent piety, as to any human phenomenon
is, ultimately speaking, peremptory. At most, one's reac
tion merely testifies to prudential differences of opinion
respecting the "goodness" or "badness" of what men do
If, however, divine revelation provides some kind of ob
jective clue to the final truth about human life, it follows

that individual judgments may cease to be equally arbitrary.

The Christian faith is committed to the second alternative, a view which must always seem presumptuous to the thinking outsider. It is indeed a presumptuous position, if it is not true. Christian faith claims, however, that its insight into the character and purpose of God and hence into the nature of the abundant life for men is not a human achievement. The assertion is made that for all the eternal mystery of the divine, a genuine word from God is embodied in the Christian gospel. One result of this claim is to chasten every human claim to absolute truth; in this respect, the Christian position possesses rational force. Yet, the Christian claim is never finally proved in this way. In the last resort, it is a venture of faith.

There is substantial agreement among Christians that the Bible provides a valid record of God's revelation to men. The interpretation of Christian faith represented here is oriented to the scriptural documents, and particularly to those of the New Testament. The biblical books are not held to possess literal inerrancy but they are taken very seriously. Let us consider the problem of the biblical attitude to religion.

No Axe to Grind for Religion

It must be made clear—and we speak quite descriptively at this point—that there is no scriptural warrant for any automatic approval of religion.

The word "religion" as it is used today is not really a biblical term at all.[9] This in itself bears upon our problem. From the scriptural point of view, religion is not a separate category of life which remains silent about the "rest" of life any more than it is an area immune to judgment by the "rest" of life. The Bible has much to say in judgment upon the religious practices of men. Whether such practices contribute to the faith in God which the Bible regards as the pearl of great price is always highly problematic. Does religious behavior accompany faith, as a spontaneous expression of trust in God, or does it stand in the way of faith? The latter possibility is just as real as the former.[10]

Hendrik Kraemer, the Dutch theologian and church leader, is true to the biblical position when he emphasizes the good-and-evil in religion as a whole—including historical and empirical Christianity. Religion is at once "creative and destructive, salutary and corruptive, sublime and demonic. It may be a source of healthy life, but may also produce illness and neurosis." The quest for salvation, liberty, happiness, ultimate truth, union with God, and victory over evil points to the elevating and liberating power in religion. One is inevitably impressed by the "superb and imposing sincerity" which religion calls out in men. Yet, the other side of the matter is equally plain. The most abhorrent and criminal deeds have been and still are associated with religion.[11]

Is it sacrilegious to be critical of religion? The fact is that some of the most thoroughgoing indictments of religion have been offered in behalf of the living God by such spokesmen as the Hebrew prophets and Jesus of Nazareth. For these men religion itself can become an affront to the name of God. It is significant that this affront is evaluated from a radically moral perspective.

I hate, I despise your feasts, and I take no delight in your solemn assemblies. Even though you offer me your burnt offerings and cereal offerings, I will not accept them, and the peace offerings of your fatted beasts I will not look upon. Take away from me the noise of your songs; to the melody of your harps I will not listen. But let justice roll down like waters, and righteousness like an ever-flowing stream.[12]

Woe to you, scribes and Pharisees, hypocrites! for you tithe mint and dill and cummin, and have neglected the weightier matters of the law, justice and mercy and faith; these you ought to have done, without neglecting the others.[13]

From the standpoint of these spokesmen, the corruption of religion is offensive in the sight of God not because his feelings are easily hurt but because false religion, by means of the debasement of human character and man's inhumanity to man, violates the created order of things. The social and the theological sides of the matter converge when religion becomes an instrument for the sin of identifying an individual's or a group's own interests with the will of God, a practice which so often entails hostility toward, and maltreatment of, other human beings. If religion should really serve human welfare, we are well advised to support one of the Bible's fundamental emphases, which was to become a cardinal tenet of the Christian social gospel: the judgment against religion itself. Failure at this latter point is a common deficiency in most of the forms of piety we have surveyed in this study.

When we apply the spirit of the Bible to the evaluation of religion and, more specifically, of the various forms of recent piety, our perspective must undergo serious transformation:

We reflect with Paul Hutchinson that "some of the currently popular types of preaching come perilously close to the blasphemy of promising success in the marketplace or an easy resolution of life's crises as a reward for calling upon God." [14]

We remember that Christian faith is not a dose of prescribed pills, one to be taken after each meal and two at bedtime, so that a man will wake up the next morning prepared to be more adjusted than he was the day before.

We recall Hendrik Kraemer's response to a verbal query whether a revival of faith is under way in Europe. Kraemer answered, "Why, perhaps there is. Church attendance seems to be decreasing." To estimate the ebb and flow of faith is always an elusive matter. Yet, there may well have been as much truth as jest in Kraemer's reply.

We wonder whether in America the fifties have been particularly faithful or whether they have simply abounded in religiosity. The god of folk religion is more often a domesticated deity than the living Lord of hosts before whom there is nothing to do but bow in contrition and thankfulness.

We are reminded of one of the lessons of Christian history—that abiding faith often needs the soil of adverse circumstance. Allegedly favorable conditions may produce no more than religiosity or perhaps forms of religion that merely praise man and his works.

And we realize, too, how the biblical outlook has not left itself without witnesses in ostensibly "secular" quarters. Thus, William H. Whyte, Jr., brings the prophet Amos down to date:

Life, as it is, is beautiful enough, and one could easily gather from current reading that God is so merged with society that the two are just about indistinguishable. In an advertisement for the movie, *A Man Called Peter,* there is a picture of a man walking up a hill through some dry-ice mist. In his white shirt and four-in-hand tie, he looks uncommonly like a thoughtful young executive, but we find that he is a minister: *"He was a first-name kind of guy. . . . He was everybody's kind of guy.*

. . . He unpomped the pompous, played baseball with kids, turned a two-hour leave into a honeymoon for a sailor and his girl, and gave voice to all the longings in a man's soul. . . . *He was a lovin' kind of guy.* . . . Every woman secretly had her eyes on him, but he had eyes for only one—Catherine—who learned from him what a wonderful thing it was to be a woman —and wrote this story that topped the nation's best-seller list for 128 weeks. . . . *He was God's kind of guy.*"

This profanity, for that is what it is, is bold, even for the popular press, but it is characteristic. God likes regular people —people who play baseball, like movie nuns. He smiles on society, and his message is a relaxing one. He does not scold you; he does not demand of you. He is a gregarious God and he can be found in the smiling happy people of the society about you. As the advertisements put it, religion can be fun.[15]

Utility Versus Purity

We are brought to consider a fundamental perplexity that has been in the background of this study as a whole and particularly the discussion so far in this chapter, the issue of a utilitarian versus a non-utilitarian application of faith.

The polar opposite of folk religion—a contrast which, to be sure, does not often appear in pure form—is the restriction of religion to the *adoratio dei*, a steady devotion and service to the Divine that may one day be consummated fully in the "beatific vision." From this point of view, the only tangible bearing that faith will have upon practical affairs derives from its antagonism to various forms of human idolatry, or illicit devotion to self, class, nation, and so on.

In folk religion, by contrast, immediate utility for men gives faith its essential quality. And yet, once men follow the lure of folk piety, how are they to avoid the practical idolatry or sacrilege of turning God into their "omnipotent servant"? Piety then becomes impiety. If, however, they retain pure faith as their ideal, will not their faith tend to be deprived, in effect, of any decisive relevance to human affairs and of any substantial meaning for the concrete problems of human life?

It is our conviction that there is a resource within the Christian faith which can permit men to be socially responsible precisely from the perspective of Christian faith itself. Is this to insinuate that we have decided to sell out? In a day when utilitarian understandings of faith appear on all sides, theology itself may incline to jump on the bandwagon. The late Bishop Francis J. McConnell once made a study in which he offered the thesis that the theology of any one period mirrors the thinking of the masses in that time. This is a disturbing possibility. It is not easy for the theologian to maintain an independent stand, especially when he looks upon part of his own task as that of helping men overcome the kind of independence that does them hurt. But before the reader conclude that we have proved after all to be merely representative rather than critical of folk piety, we beg him to postpone his final judgment at least until the theological basis of our position has been expressed.

For some time the center of our own theological reasoning has itself been the need for judgment against different forms of human idolatry. Although we have sensed for a while the inadequacies in this criterion at the point of positive moral action, we were recently brought up short by a passage from the pen of Reinhold Niebuhr, included as part of a book review containing a criticism of Paul Tillich. Niebuhr takes as his point of departure Tillich's well-known insistence that the chief objective criterion of ultimate truth is that the God of our devotion is the very ground of all things rather than a being beside other beings. Niebuhr says:

. . . This insistence, which comes to terms with all idolatrous distortions of faith, in which men are ultimately concerned with nation, success or some other ephemeral end or value, naturally places mystic religions, with their rigorous rejection of all the relative ends of history, and Biblical faith, with its hazardous but creative dealing with the stuff of historical responsibilities, on a par. It may also fail to do justice to the particular meaning and purpose of the divine assigned to the divine in the Christian revelation, particularly in the assertion that "God was in Christ reconciling the world unto himself." This is to say that the Christian faith is ultimately concerned, not with worshipping the mystery if it is but the mystery of the reconciliation between the divine purpose and the fragmentary and idolatrous human purposes. In other words *it is concerned, not in evading idolatry, but in accepting historic responsibilities with an easy and yet uneasy conscience, since every form of human striving is bound to be idolatrous in the ultimate court. One might say that ideally the Christian faith enables men, not to escape idolatry absolutely, but to accept responsibilities, knowing that those responsibilities will involve us in idolatries from which no form of human perfection will redeem us.* This is the meaning of Luther's admonition, "Sin bravely if also you have brave faith." This is also the meaning of the Reformation's rejection of the ascetic effort to bridge the chasm between the divine and the human by strenuous human effort. The insistence on divine mercy as the final answer to the human predicament does not absolve us of responsibility but frees us for performing tasks in a world which never confronts us with clear choices of good and evil.[16]

Human resources are incapable of resolving the dilemma of religious utility versus religious purity. From a human standpoint alone, men are indeed driven back and forth between the idolatries that accompany responsible action and the moral irresponsibilities that arise out of the justifiable fear of making idols of "worldly" causes. But it is the Christian faith that God acts to meet human extremity and to save perplexed men from despair. The gift that men can receive is the divine mercy through Jesus Christ. This resource permits them to face up to their dilemmas with perseverance and hope. When men take their stand upon the divine forgiveness, they are enabled to ground the life of morality upon the life of faith. Through the power of forgiveness as the ultimate resource of the Christian faith men are delivered both from irresponsibility and from the reduction of religion to a mere system of morality. As Reinhold Niebuhr has stated elsewhere, the gospel of forgiveness "proves itself not a panacea for all the world's ills but an ultimate comfort to those who scorn the comfort of illusions about themselves." Emancipated from such illusions, men today may be empowered to co-operate with other men in seeking tolerable solutions for the insurmountable problems of our time.[17] In this way the Christian faith becomes directly relevant to the fundamental practical problems that men face in this world.

The Christian question is this: In the presence of God as revealed in Christ, how can we be most responsible? We are called to responsibility within the form and content of our own lives and in all relations with our brothers. Men like Norman Vincent Peale and Billy Graham, through their own personal efforts, teach us much about the life of Christian responsibility. But the self-demanding aspects of the Peale message and, to a lesser extent, of the Graham message must not be allowed to produce the vain hope of an expected human perfection. The responsibility we commend looks to the divine mercy for the final resolution of our predicament and hence for the freedom "wherewith Christ hath made us free"—a freedom which can issue in responsible moral and social action.

We are led to conclude that the Christian faith is not required to turn its back upon utilitarian applications of faith. Christians themselves can and will seek to realize the highest degree of moral responsibility.

Our New Gospels, the Social Gospel, and the Whole Gospel

We face a further dilemma that parallels in considerable measure the one just considered. Stated extremely, the dilemma is one of a gospel addressed to individuals in their discreteness versus a gospel addressed to life at the collective level. Is "personal salvation" or "social salvation" the primary Christian goal?

The temptation for the latter alternative is to become, in a phrase of H. Richard Niebuhr, all "social" and no "gospel." The temptation for the former emphasis is to be all "gospel" while remaining oblivious to, or unconcerned about, problems posed for faith by the communal life of men. As a matter of fact, representatives of the "personal gospel" have often expressed honest fear that the "social gospel" is a corrupting influence upon the true meaning of Christian faith. From the perspective of a unilaterally individualist understanding of faith, when religious men come to act concertedly in secular life, as act all men must in one way or another, it is not as men of faith but as citizens that they will see themselves making a contribution.[18]

We believe that the "social gospel" in the Christian church is not, in principle, tempted *by something within its own convictions* to lose sight of the independent significance of personal conversion. This is said in relative contrast to a tendency within the individualist approach to be unable to provide for a responsible and effective love of neighbor. (The command to love the neighbor may not, in and of its precise wording, demand the social application of Christian faith; yet the question has long been raised among Christians whether love as an act can have real substance apart from action upon the social situation.) Concern for social issues, in so far as it is a Christian concern, finds its *motivation* in personal commitment to Christ. On the other hand, commitment to Christ in behalf of a strongly "personal gospel"—even a commitment which is, from all evidences, the most genuine possible— may still fail to attain a social outreach.

The evaluation above is not intended to imply absolute differences between the two approaches. The basic problem concerns the relative moral expectations we may have for each view. The race question in America is a case in point. The cult of reassurance simply ignores the question. The new revivalism's "answer" is the same as its answer to all serious moral issues: the conversion of the heart of the individual to Christ. The gospel of group interest, as typified in International Christian Leadership, does not address itself directly to this question. If it did, then, on the basis of its general pronouncements, its strategy would no doubt duplicate the individualist strategy of Billy Graham. Graham's approach does go one step further than most other approaches. He refers to the Church's service in creating a climate of good will and in providing a place in which the individual Christian can "take a stand for neighbor-love." [19] Nor does Graham permit religion to underwrite the racial *status quo*. Nevertheless, in Graham's position, as in the others, the instrumentality of Christian social action is cut off.

The influence of most of the religious leadership we have been considering in this study is hardly in the direction of a *revival* of religion if by this is meant instilling new wine into fresh wineskins. The truth is that a stress upon subjective, individual religion is a throwback to an earlier day. Social Christianity, as a partner of personal Christian faith, has been one of the momentous achievements of the churches in the twentieth century. This view has emphasized that, without fundamental provision for dealing with life in society, the Christian gospel fails to address itself to human life as it is actually lived.

Many Christians are much disturbed by any version of Christian faith which is deficient at the point of moral and social responsibility in the here and now. For them, the phrase "bring men to Christ" has a hollow and futile ring apart from such responsibility. They believe that the Christian life means taking with utmost seriousness the life of one who "went about doing good" [20]—with such seriousness, in fact, that they refuse to exempt any segment of social life from searching criticism and reforming action from the point of view of Christian faith. They understand too that men are not "souls" in abstraction from "bodies" but that the material and physical aspects of life are integral to human spirituality. They are convinced, in short, that human existence is both individual and social and that human personality is a unity of body and spirit. In this persuasion they help to carry forward the biblical understanding of the character of human life.

It would appear that the fortunes of the twentieth century have confirmed the insistence of Christian social thinkers that on the one hand, the structures of evil in society are too powerful for individual men, no matter how regenerate and numerous, to overcome, and, on the other hand, that it remains possible to carry on constructive social action. Underlying both points is the Christian affirmation—fragmentarily recognized and unconsciously supported by some facets of folk religion—that men are made for life in community.

When we refer to constructive social action, we do not imply any dream of building the kingdom of God on earth. Utopianism as a strain in Christian thinking has been so long dead—apart from sporadic resurrections in a spokesman like Billy Graham—that it is hardly necessary to bury it all over again. A group succeeds, say, in a fight for better housing. The people move out of the slums— only to end up in the conformities of a great housing project. Social justice may compound its own problems. William H. Whyte, Jr., is quite correct that

the fruits of social revolution are always more desirable in anticipation than fact, and the pink lamp shade in the picture window can be a sore disappointment to those who dreamed that the emancipation of the worker would take a more spiritual turn.[21]

Whyte continues that it is a sight which men, nevertheless, can well endure. He refers to the fact that "acclimatization to the middle class will lessen the feeling of social vulnerability" that can turn people ugly. There is considerable truth in the view which claims, in a way not unlike Paul's attitude to the Hebrew Law, that minimally considered, social reform functions as a means of restraining sin.

The restraint of sin is not, however, the only rationale of moral effort. Since it is impossible to separate the lives of individual men from life in society, and the material aspect of life from the spiritual aspect, social action ought always to be a constituent part of the missionary activity of the Church. Nevertheless, there is no necessity to conclude that where social action in behalf of human beings does not prove "successful," it ought to cease. Christians may seek to love their neighbors as themselves and, in terms of tangible approximations to the good society, actually get nowhere. The question they must continually ask is not how much they may achieve but how they may be most responsible. The Christian ethic of forgiveness may emancipate men from the limiting motivation of practical success. Further, Christians are never without the assurance that in strange and impenetrable ways, their efforts are finally gathered up into the divine purpose. They are spared the disillusionment that must finally come to those whose policies for action must result in positive achievement in order to merit continued support.

According to the First Letter of John, if men say they have fellowship with God, yet are actually estranged from their brothers, they are guilty of sin. But in so far as they love their brothers, they are brought thereby into the light of God. Indeed, the man "who does not love his brother whom he has seen, cannot love God whom he has not seen." [22] To assert that one can truly love God apart from love of the neighbor is to fall into an abstraction, a selfish allegation devoid of living meaning and content.

We do not imply that personal devotion to God is incapable of providing Christian social action with meaning and power. It is, on the contrary, the very love of God that should issue in love of neighbor. The type of pietist

faith which, as in the Wesleyan movement, finally culmi-
nates in concerted social action is actually quite a different
matter from the individualist religion that inclines to
move on a wholly personal plane above such allegedly
dubious enterprises as politics. Psychologically speaking,
the fact that God-centered piety has often reached fulfillment in social applications of the gospel provides good
evidence that in their total spiritual pilgrimage the "pious
souls" in question had never completely cast off the bond
of brotherhood.

The fact remains that we cannot use the device of in-
specting alternative religious presuppositions in either
theoretical or biographical terms in order to calculate precisely which form of faith is going to be most responsible
morally and socially. Time and again men behave in ways
that transcend their patterns of belief and their erstwhile
historical experience. Thus, there is no foolproof guarantee that Christian concentration upon the social outreach
of faith will not lapse into outright folk religion or even
finally end in the apostasy of humanistic secularism. Men
can hardly be relied upon to stand fast in their allegiance
to the true God. It is all too easy for human beings to
come to find the meaning of their existence in some finite
cause and in their contributions to it, with the result that
they are sore beset to avoid celebrating their own virtue.

Nevertheless, once again the central consideration for
Christians is not that of the ways of men with their fellows
or even that of the ways of men with God. The real issue
concerns both the ways of God with men and God's rightful place of honor in the universe he has made. Concern
with human life in society is saved from becoming "all
social and no gospel" *to the extent that* Christians remember, first, that the primary motivation of Christian ethics

is gratitude to God for his love [23] and, second, that God
is the only intrinsic value in the whole world. In the
double commandment affirmed or confirmed by Jesus,

it is only God who is to be loved with heart, soul, mind and
strength; the neighbor is put on the same level of value that
the self occupies. . . . The value of man, like the value of
sparrow and flower, is his value to God. . . . Christ loves his
neighbor not as he loves himself but as God loves him. Hence
the Fourth Gospel, discerning that the Jewish statement "Love
thy neighbor as thyself" fitted adequately neither Jesus' actions
nor his requirements, changed the commandment to read,
"Love one another as I have loved you." . . . [We must recog-
nize] that what the early Christians saw in Jesus Christ, and
what we must accept if we look at him rather than at our
imaginations about him, was not a person characterized by
universal benignity, loving God and man. His love of God and
his love of neighbor are two distinct virtues that have no common quality but only a common source. Love of God is adora-
tion of the only true good; it is gratitude to the bestower of
all gifts; it is joy in Holiness; it is "consent to Being." But the
love of man is pitiful rather than adoring; it is giving and for-
giving rather than grateful; it suffers for and in their vicious-
ness and profaneness; it does not consent to accept them as
they are, but calls them to repentance. . . .
   . . . The Christ of the New Testament possesses [the virtues
of love, faith and humility]. . . . But he practices none of them
and requires none of them of his followers otherwise than in
relation to God. . . .
   . . . [Christ] does not direct attention away from this world
to another; but from all worlds, present and future, material
and spiritual, to the One who creates all worlds, who is the
Other of all worlds.[24]

Christian love of the neighbor presupposes the truth
that the same God who loves the believer also loves his

neighbors, just as it rests too upon the truth already mentioned that true love for God is empty apart from love of neighbor.

We are led to a final consideration, of relevance to the present section. If God in Christ saves the *world* in a total sense, the Christian gospel thereby relates itself to all of human existence in a way that transcends mere social relationships. The social gospel derives its sustenance and its value from the Christian gospel in its wholeness. If the new gospels of our day are socially deficient, the social gospel joins these other gospels in being Christianly deficient until all are subject to the whole gospel.

It is one thing, often a good thing, to lift up a particular facet of faith for concerted attention, especially when that facet has been subject to neglect. It is quite another thing to proceed as though that single emphasis—spiritual and psychological wholeness, repentance for sin, the use of capacities for leadership, the need for social and economic reform—were the one and only treasure of the Christian gospel. To do that is to jeopardize one's partial contribution.

Many forms of the recent piety trespass, in varied ways, upon the wholeness of the Christian faith. The only way that this state of affairs can be transformed is in and through the corporate Christian church, the Body of Christ, which God has called out from all nations to serve as the peculiar witness of his majesty, judgment, forgiveness, and love to the whole world.[25] The task that gives the Church its meaning is the evangelical task, a responsibility with multiple dimensions.

Evangelism is . . . a continuing task in many varied forms: prophetic and homiletic witness; theological clarification, inquiry, and defense; formal and informal nurture, Biblical and catechetical teaching; corporate and individual counseling—all to the end that God in Christ may be more clearly, fully, and powerfully known.[26]

Loyalty to the whole gospel is a preventive of simplification and, consequently, of irony in religion. It is a pity that with mass attention to such leaders as Messrs. Peale and Graham, the American public, already grievously ignorant in matters religious, may be led to confuse these manifestations of piety with the whole Christian gospel. Churchmen who have reservations about the most recent forms of piety ought, accordingly, to voice their convictions through all possible means. By doing so, they help to fulfill their own responsibilities for evangelism.

On the Resolution of Human Problems

Early in Chapter Two attention was called to a dominant theme in folk piety—the persuasion that religion is a deliverer. At several points in the present chapter reference is made to grounds for a pragmatic application of faith. Are we led to conclude that the primary function of faith is to resolve basic human problems of a personal and social sort? With the material so far presented in this chapter as background, what may we say more specifically and systematically respecting the claim that religion is a deliverer? It would be indeed ironic for our entire analysis if the presentation did no more than reflect the point of view of folk religion.

If outright superstition is to be avoided, "faith," "belief," and "religion" are clearly not entities in themselves. Further, if the faith men are being widely urged to have really comes down to reliance upon themselves, it would clear the air considerably—although it might be too much to expect—if those who think this way would simply come out and say that it is man in whom people ought to have increasing faith. What other connotation than this can be placed upon the particular counsel of Norman Vincent Peale that men should "have faith in faith"?

In the presence of this humanistic claim, two types of response are in order. First, is there really ground for hope that men are able to resolve their problems through such devices as are found in the several forms of the new piety? Serious reservations about an affirmative reply are found in the tradition of biblical and Protestant faith. Second and more important, there is the question—at once ethical, psychological, and theological—of what is the legitimacy in employing religion as an ideological cloak under which man, in effect, is devoted to himself and to his own resources. As William Lee Miller puts it, if the object of devotion is "religion" rather than God, the resulting religiosity easily becomes the instrument of a more substantial commitment, the commitment to man's own purposes.[27]

If, on the other hand, the reaction is forthcoming that the saving resources available are other than purely human ones, at least three major alternatives now present themselves:

1. The faith that is advocated means the hope that by some mysterious good fortune the course of natural events will come out on man's side if he will just push things a bit and carry his share of the load.

Against this alternative one need only make the obvious, if melancholy, point that although the course of natural events bestows much of promise and beauty upon man, it also does him in at the last, whether he pushes things or not.

2. The faith which is asseverated can conceivably be directed to a number of gods.

Although it is probably true that practically speaking, there is much polytheism in American popular piety—now happiness, now the social *status quo,* now faith itself seeks to compel men's devotion—not many Americans will consciously want to subscribe at the religious level to such a confusing and dubious alternative as this.

3. Faith in faith is transcended, and men, now carried beyond all abstract and natural forces and all finite divinities too, are brought face to face with the God beyond the gods. In the biblical view faith remains a vain thing apart from some form of concrete, living confrontation with the God of Abraham and of Jesus Christ.

If the faith men are counseled to practice implies that behind religion the Lord of the universe stands within the shadows, quite a new question is raised: Can God or will God resolve human problems? *When the issue is stated in this way, a completely negative reply to the question of the resolution of human problems through faith is not demanded from a Christian perspective, once it is insisted that the problems of men are met not on human terms but on God's.*

One immediate qualification is that the resolution of human problems is not the unitary focus of Christian faith. According to the New Testament, the center of the gospel lies in what it says about God—his creative acts in the history of the world and of men, and how he is finally disposed toward men. The New Testament is not primarily concerned with a "solution" to "problems"; instead, it turns a man's gaze to Christ in a way that can make him both strangely nonchalant about his own problems and strangely concerned for the lives of others. When Paul wrote to the Philippians from a dreadful Roman prison, the question of his own peace of mind and security was supremely irrelevant. He simply wanted to assure his brethren that the things which happened to him had actually "served to advance the gospel." [28]

This suggests another refinement of the issue of the relation of religion and human problems: Whose problems are involved? In Christian faith a man may be assigned greater problems than he ever had before, only to have them removed at last through the paradox of the life that is found through losing itself.

The biblical outlook as a whole is echoed in that aspect of the cult of reassurance which, in Paul Hutchinson's description, maintains that the human story makes sense. Much popular piety is crude. To say with Jane Russell, one of Hollywood's younger theologians, that the Lord is a "livin' Doll" is to live close to sacrilege. But the familiarity with God that may breed contempt in others also points up the fact that for many ingenuous and less reflective souls, the only other viable alternative to faith would be a hopeless realization that the universe has not the slightest interest in what happens to human beings. Thus, from one point of view Jane Russell's phrase provides a triumphant contrast to Macbeth's despairing conclusion,

> Life's but a walking shadow, a poor player,
> That struts and frets his hour upon the stage,
> And then is heard no more; it is a tale
> Told by an idiot, full of sound and fury,
> Signifying nothing.

We must continue to insist, however, that on the biblical view, the human story makes sense because it comes

out, not of necessity where men want it to come out—for
that might not be real sense—but because it comes out
where God intends it to come out. God knows what is
good for men in ways considerably hidden to human sight.
Knowledge of this fact is precisely the resource that raises
men to a vantage point beyond human irony, pathos, and
tragedy.

It is presumed in this study that a Christian norm for
personality is some kind of tension between healthy-
minded and sick-souled elements. Men may rejoice in God
as creator and redeemer; they must lament the tragedies
of life and their own inadequacies and sin. It has been
well said that the function of Christian preaching is to
comfort the afflicted and to afflict the comfortable. This
provides American Christianity with at least two main
strategies of faith. Through the gospel of divine comfort
and mercy, the Christian faith may bring victory over the
afflictions of self-centeredness and despair. Through the
gospel of divine judgment, the Christian faith may afflict
men in their comforts—not merely the things of this world
that capture their allegiance but also the superficial and
self-satisfied comforts exemplified in the cult of reassurance itself.

These two alternatives are not either-or choices. They
are twin responsibilities. The Christian gospel in its wholeness permits of no separation of mercy from judgment, of
love from wrath. The "afflicted" and the "comfortable"
are most often one and the same man. Ultimately, every
human being hungers for both assurance and challenge,
forgiveness and demand. Judgment without love is cold
retribution; love without judgment is sentimentality.
Christian faith overcomes the fear that cringes before

naked divine power and the self-indulgence that saps character and integrity.

Billy Graham maintains that "spiritual revival comes when God's people meet His conditions." From a biblical point of view, this "if-then" interpretation of God's action is not in itself a mistaken one. There is, indeed, an element of contingency in the biblical apprehension of the divine life. The parties to the Covenant between God and man certainly influence one another. The relation is understood in highly mutual and personal terms. However, the understanding of God as a personal, responding being is a two-edged sword. God responds in ways that meet the deep needs of men, to be sure. But as the creator of men God alone knows the final meaning of their needs and the final disposition that must be made of these needs. If God is truly personal and free, he may respond in a manner quite dissimilar to anything man can hope for or conceive. Though it is true in principle that if men satisfy the right conditions, God will respond, the stubborn fact is that amidst the complexities of a good-and-evil world and the curious mixtures in their own motives, men can never be certain what are the right conditions and whether they are satisfying them.

From a Christian perspective, it would be absurd to censure Norman Vincent Peale for maintaining the reality of divine power in the world. The trouble lies rather in Peale's presupposition that the individual can without any material reservation consistently appropriate that power for his own personal and immediate interests. It would appear that on the Peale view, God is more an automatically operating machine than he is a responsible, personal being, and more the servant of man than the sovereign creator and judge of all things.

According to the Christian faith, the surest indication of the nature of God and, hence, of what are the "divine conditions" for the abundant life of which Billy Graham speaks is found, of course, in the person and the acts of Jesus Christ. It must be emphasized, however, that neither in his teachings nor in his acts does Jesus furnish exact laws of moral and religious action. He provides instead principles for action which are to be applied responsibly yet always venturesomely amidst the confusions and challenges of the common life of men. Jesus' love commandment means "a practical disposition or attitude which is to manifest itself in many different kinds of acts according to the needs of particular situations." His precepts disclose the quality and direction the Christian's actions ought to take under all circumstances.[29]

The Christian tradition has agreed that Jesus' teachings and actions are in some way exemplary for men. It has insisted with equal force that Jesus is the judge of men, even when they are earnestly seeking to follow him as their example. There is nothing in either Jesus' precepts or the events of his death and resurrection to spare the disciple uncertainty—other than the assurance that whatsoever things are just and gracious are finally vindicated and God's will is finally done. Men can have faith in Jesus Christ, but they may not use him, much less their own partial insight, as a slide rule for calculating the conditions by virtue of which God is certain to act in such and such a way. It was Jesus himself who prayed, "Nevertheless, not as I will, but as thou wilt." [30] Herein lies the peace of God. The partners in the Covenant are not equal partners. Only God knows what is ultimately best for men. It is on his own terms that he resolves their problems.

A Summary Reckoning

Is it really true that human beings constitute the final cause and the absolute value in this world? If the answer is yes, then there is nothing inherently wrong with folk religion. Such piety can be accepted as a useful means for discovering and promoting what is really valuable. Should a particular brand of folk religion fail to achieve what is calculated for it, it can always be revised and improved, without any surrender of the point of view of folk religion itself.

But if, on the contrary, the final cause or the center of all value in this world is not man but God, then folk religion stands under an awesome judgment. If, as the Christian faith maintains, the will of God is man's only final peace, then folk religion is in and of itself an affront not merely to God but to human dignity and well-being as well. We cannot emphasize too strongly here our conviction that the fault of folk religion is *not* that it is, as such, too centered in man. The trouble is, instead, that when man is exalted after the fashion of folk religion, that form of religion turns out to be his enemy. We are enabled, in consequence, to meet the apostles of folk religion on their own ground. Whenever man makes himself the center of existence, he becomes alienated from himself. To give the honor and glory to One not himself is to receive fullness of life. As Augustine came to know, men do not reach a final rest until they find their rest in the God who made them. This is how Christians are enabled to refer to their faith as, in Jacques Maritain's phrase, an *integral humanism*, a true humanism. And this is the primary indictment of folk religion by Christian faith.

Disputation Taken Captive by Love

There remains, however, one other side to the matter. We refer to the issue of the self-humiliation of God. This question cannot be passed by.

When for all practical purposes folk religion casts God in the role of a servant of man, we must say that the assigning of this role *by men* is illicit. Even from within a Christian perspective, men cannot pretend that it is their importance which induces the humbling of God for their sakes. Nevertheless, Christians are able to affirm, by faith, that the role of the Divine as the servant of man is a real one and is, indeed, the very ground of their salvation. The New Testament dares to make the claim that *God does humble himself for them.* At this decisive juncture we cannot be too grateful for Christ-centered elements in the witness of Billy Graham.

It is by faith alone that men are permitted to speak of God's service to man. Otherwise, any such assertion would be blasphemous. The gift of Christ is not the basis of a claim upon God. The coming of Christ would then cease to be a gift and would become a center of judgment against man. Human claims are annulled in the Crucifixion. The self-humiliation of God in the person of the Son can be separated neither from the person of the Father nor from the person of the Spirit in all his *holiness.* Only God can say that he will sacrifice himself for men. But this is as it should be because only God can accomplish the deed his word promises. There is all the difference in the world between this divine decision and any claim on the part of men that God must necessarily act in this or any way. Yet, once all these reservations are offered—reservations made so terribly necessary by the fact that man stands here within the holy of holies—the simple and miraculous truth remains that the sovereign Lord of all things does will to serve men. He for whom the far reaches of space and time are casual affairs kneels before his creatures and washes their feet.

The most sublime level of faith is the divine forgiveness, for at last men are given an answer to a problem before which their own resources totally fail. It is the problem of guilt. They have no answer of their own, because it is they who make the accusation against themselves. *Is there someone out there in the great world who still cares?* If there is an answer, Christian faith is a witness to the only possible one. Man's courage to affirm himself in spite of the anxiety of guilt is rooted in the mercy of God. The Christian knows himself as at once sinful and yet justified, unacceptable and yet accepted.[31] He cannot insist that God forgive him. Yet God does humble himself for the sake of men. The New Testament message that "Christ died for our sins" is addressed to all. Peace of mind advocates, now-or-never revivalists, religious nationalists, Christian libertarians, social conformists, and, as those born out of due time, perhaps even critics of the surge of American piety can be brought with saints, martyrs, and an uncounted company of souls into the fellowship of an incredible democracy. Its foundation is the living God, who lays down his life for every member.

Notes

1. Will Herberg, "Faith and Character Structure," *Christianity and Crisis*, Jan. 25, 1954, pp. 188, 189. By permission of *Christianity and Crisis*.

2. *Ibid.*

3. The other side of this point is that in principle, the less readily that envy can be attributed to a critic, the more seriously we may listen to what he has to say. We all have our psychological problems but it becomes rather ludicrous to psychoanalyze men of the stature of Reinhold Niebuhr into really wishing that they were Billy Graham.

4. I Corinthians 1:21.

5. Romans 2:1 (RSV).

6. Isaiah 55:8 (RSV).

7. Psalms 76:10 (RSV).

8. From a letter to *The Christian Century* (issue of Dec. 8, 1954) by C. F. Avey, in criticism of the present writer's original article on the general subject under discussion.

9. Alan Richardson, ed., *A Theological Word Book of the Bible* (New York: The Macmillan Company, 1952), p. 188.

10. It may be noted that the most unsophisticated individual is often aware that what other people do and say religiously need not be identical with the will of God. When the individual goes on from this awareness to make the common charge of hypocrisy against church people, we are not forced to dismiss his charge as no more than reprehensible self-righteousness. In so far as men persist in making tacit distinctions between human claims and the will of God, we are saved from complete despair over humanity's spiritual state.

11. Hendrik Kraemer, *Religion and the Christian Faith* (London: Lutterworth Press, 1956), pp. 38-39.

12. Amos 5:21-24 (RSV).

13. Matthew 23:23 (RSV).

14. Paul Hutchinson, *The New Ordeal of Christianity* (New York: Association Press, 1957), p. 112.

15. From *The Organization Man,* by William H. Whyte, Jr. (New York: Simon and Schuster, Inc., 1956), p. 254. By permission of Simon and Schuster, Inc.

16. Reinhold Niebuhr, review of Paul Tillich's *Dynamics of Faith,* *Union Seminary Quarterly Review,* May, 1957, p. 112. The italics are added. Used by permission of *Union Seminary Quarterly Review.*

17. Reinhold Niebuhr "After Comment, the Deluge," *The Christian Century, op. cit.,* pp. 1034, 1035.

18. This position is somewhat reminiscent of the one traditionally associated—not with one hundred per cent validity—with classical Lutheranism.

19. "Billy Graham Makes Plea for an End to Intolerance," *Life,* Oct. 1, 1956, pp. 138-151.

20. Acts 10:38.

21. Whyte, *op. cit.,* pp. 309-310.

22. I John 1:6; 2:10; 4:20.

23. I John 4:19.

24. H. Richard Niebuhr, *Christ and Culture* (New York: Harper & Brothers, 1951), pp. 17, 18, 19, 28. By permission of Harper & Brothers.

25. Charles Clayton Morrison, "The Past Foreshadows the Future," *The Christian Century,* March 5, 1958, p. 274.

26. *The Good News of God: The Nature and Task of Evangelism,* Report of a special commission of the National Council of the Churches of Christ in the U.S.A. (New York: National Council of the Churches of Christ in the U.S.A., 1957), pp. 16-17. It would be uncharitable to omit the fact that Norman Vincent Peale was a member of this commission.

27. Miller, "Piety Along the Potomac," *op. cit.,* p. 27.

28. Philippians 1:12 (RSV).

29. George F. Thomas, *Christian Ethics and Moral Philosophy* (New York: Charles Scribner's Sons, 1955), pp. 39, 40.

30. Matthew 26:39.

31. Paul Tillich, *The Courage to Be* (New Haven: Yale University Press, 1952), p. 164.

Index

America: and cult of nation, 126-127, 159; cultural pluralism in, 58; as melting pot, 35, 36, 56; religio-political tradition of, 53-58, 132; *see also under* American people, American religion, "American way of life," Folk religion

American Institute of Public Opinion, 39, 40

American people: attitudes to religion of, 154-155; and materialism, 122-123; optimism of, 28-29, 55, 87; "third generation" of, 34, 35-36; *see also* Folk religion, Individualism

American religion: and American tradition, 34, 53-57, 146; main forms of, 35, 36, 56, 58, 59; assumptions in, 61-64, 74; uniqueness of, 32-38; *see also under* Folk religion, Piety, the new, Secularism

"American way of life," 51, 58, 59-61, 87

Anxiety: and religion, 27-30, 32-33, 73-75

Atheism, 25: and Christian faith, 149

Augustine, 184

Avey, C. F., 187

Beauvoir, de, Simone, 122

Bennett, John C., 66-67, 104, 116

Berdyaev, Nicolas, 123

Bible: and religion, 161-165; Christian estimate of, 105, 161; *see also under* Fundamentalism, New Testament

Brauer, Jerald C., 101-102, 116

Buttrick, George A., 147

Calvinism, 128, 130

Catholicism, 35, 40, 57

Christian Century, The, 11, 96-97, 110-111, 116, 117, 118, 143-144, 145, 152

Christian Economics, 48, 128-129, 134

Christian faith: center of, 98-101; and fundamentalism, 105-106; as good news, 97-98; and idolatry, 126, 166-168; and materialism, 123; and meaning of life, 180-181; and peace of mind, 179-180; and personality norms, 181; and resolution of human problems, 121, 177-183; and social responsibility, 166-

189

176; wholeness of, 176-177, 181;
see also under Christian life,
Church, God, Jesus Christ

Christian Freedom Foundation, 48,
119, 124, 128, 139

Christian life, basis of, 98, 166-169,
171, 173-174, 174-175; *see also under* Christian faith, Church, Love
of neighbor, Social gospel

Church: and Billy Graham, 115; as
Body of Christ, 108, 147, 148, 176;
evangelism and, 106, 176-177; failure of, 147-148; and individual,
146-149; modern attitude to, 114;
strategies of, 181-182; and whole
gospel, 176-177; *see also under*
Social gospel

Church and state, 54, 56

Church attendance, reasons for, 40

Church membership: and conformity, 37; statistics on, 22-23, 40

Communism, 45-46, 84, 120, 122-123,
124, 125, 126

Conformism: and churches, 146,
148-149; trend to, 135-143, 151;
distinguished from conformity,
138, 140, 141, 142, 145, 159; and
human freedom, 142; and new
piety, 135-136, 143-146, 150, 159

Conformity; *see under* Conformism

Covenant, the, 182, 183

"Cult of reassurance," 28-29, 72, 170;
and Christian faith, 180-182; evaluation of, 73 ff.; *see also* Peale,
Norman Vincent

"Culture religion," usage of term,
42-43; *see also under* Folk religion

Democracy, 53-54, 120, 125, 128; and
Christian faith, 132-133, 134

Devil, the, 95, 116, 117

Durkheim, Émile, 127

Eastern Orthodoxy, 40-41

Easton, W. Burnet, Jr., 102-103, 116

Faith: domestication of, 57-61; in
man, 177-178; utilitarian and non-

utilitarian, 165-169; *see also under* Christian faith, God

Faith and Freedom, 47-48, 65, 128

Folk religion, 19, 67, 130, 165, 172,
174; and American tradition, 52-
57, 61-63; attractions of, 64; evaluation of, 68-69, 72, 164, 184-185;
and national interest, 72, 119-120;
nature of, 42-49; *see also under*
American religion, Piety, the new,
Religion

Forgiveness: and Christian morality,
167-168, 173; divine, 186

Fosdick, Harry Emerson, 117

Foundation for Religious Action in
the Social and Civil Order, 125-
126, 134

Freedom of man, 130-133; and
church, 146-149; religion and, 145-
146; *see also* Democracy

Freedom, religious, 38, 54, 55-56

"Free enterprise"; *see* Libertarianism

Freud, Sigmund, 73

Fromm, Erich, 78

Fundamentalism: and Billy Graham, 105-107; pietistic and scholastic, 106-107

Gallup, George, 29, 40

Gill, Theodore A., 105-106

God: as "ally" of men, 48-49, 50, 52,
64, 121-122, 125-126, 159; biblical
view of, 158, 179-183; faith in, 57,
162, 179; grace of, 103, 117, 147;
judgment of, 54, 96, 133, 150, 159,
181-182; kingdom of, 86; love of,
98, 173, 174-176; mercy of, 168,
169, 181; peace of, 86, 100, 184;
and human problems, 179-181,
182, 183; revelation of, 160-161,
183; self-humiliation of, 185-186;
and sociopolitical order, 120, 129-
130; sovereignty of, 151, 186;
transcendence of, 158-160; will of,
187

"Gospel of group interest," 119 ff.,
170

Graham, Billy, 18, 31, 49-52, 60-61, 62-63, 65, 66-67, 93-98, 100-111, 115, 116, 117, 119-120, 124, 150, 156-157, 168, 170-171, 172, 177, 182, 183, 185, 187, 188; New York City "crusade" of, 61, 94-95, 96-97, 111-113, 114, 115-116, 120, 143-144

"Healthy-mindedness," 73, 89, 181
Herberg, Will, 33-38, 40, 53, 58-60, 66, 106, 125, 134, 155-156, 186
Holy Spirit, 95, 96, 97, 100, 108, 146, 185
Hutchinson, Paul, 27-28, 29, 40, 75, 90, 91-92, 152, 163, 187

Idolatry, 96, 123, 125, 126-127, 129, 149, 165-166
Individual, dehumanization of, 137; *see also under* Church
Individualism: American ethic of, 139; in religion, 169-170, 171, 174; in socio-economic life, 127-133
"Inner-directedness," 36, 156
Intellectuals, attitudes of, 28, 65, 71-72, 102-104, 136, 137, 139, 150
International Christian Leadership, 46-48, 121, 123-124, 125, 170
Irony: usage of term, 70-71; and new piety, 149-150

James, William, 73, 89-90, 92
Jesus Christ, 86, 94, 98, 99, 100-101, 102, 109, 147, 162-163, 168, 169, 170, 175, 176, 179, 183, 185, 186
Johnson, F. Ernest, 58, 66
Judaism, 35, 36, 40, 56, 57-58

Kierkegaard, Sören, 150
Knox, John, 116
Kraemer, Hendrik, 162, 164, 187

Libertarianism, 47-48, 53, 72; evaluation of, 127-133
Love of neighbor, 170-171, 173, 175-176, 183

McConnell, Francis J., 166
Macmurray, John, 66

Man: as child of God, 142, 146; and course of nature, 178; and community, 142, 172; moral obligation of, 142, 155, 166; nature of, 89, 117, 130-133, 171; rights of, 132; *see also* Freedom of man
Maritain, Jacques, 184
Meserve, Harry C., 39
Miller, William Lee, 23, 39, 91, 134, 152, 178, 188
Morrison, Charles Clayton, 188

Negroes, 36, 80-82
New Testament, and American tradition, 53; *see also under* Bible, God, Jesus Christ, Paul
New York Times, The, 94, 115-116
Niebuhr, H. Richard, 102, 169, 188
Niebuhr, Reinhold, 55, 63, 70, 71, 72, 82, 102, 106-107, 116, 117, 149, 166-167, 168, 187, 188
Nonconformism, Christian, 148-149

Oates, Wayne E., 76-78, 87-88, 90, 91, 92
"Organization man," 138-142
"Other-directedness," 18-19, 36-37, 155-156

Paul, 172, 179-180; *cited*, 53, 66, 106, 117, 157, 187, 188
Peace of mind; *see* "Cult of reassurance"
Peale, Norman Vincent, 18, 31, 44-45, 61, 65, 75-78, 79, 80-89, 90-91, 94, 95, 97-98, 100, 119, 139, 150, 156, 160, 168, 177, 178, 182, 188
Pettingill, Samuel B., 134
Piety, the new: and church, 146-149; and communism, 122-123; description of, 42 ff.; diffusion of, 23-25, 38-39; and entertainment, 24, 38-39, 150; evaluation of, 153 ff.; and God, 158-160; and nation, 23-24, 38-39, 119-120, 126-127, 150; roots of, 26-39, 56-57, 73-75, 84; sincerity in, 69, 95, 128, 135; *see also under* American religion, Folk re-

ligion, "Gospel of group interest,"
Religion, Revivalism
Piety, usage of term, 19
Polytheism, 179
Pope, Liston, 129
Protestant Council of New York
City, and Graham crusade, 114
Protestantism, 35, 40, 57, 101
Psychology, 73-74, 76, 77-78, 79-80
Public opinion methods, 136-137
Puritan ideal, 55, 87

Race question, 81-82, 124, 170-171
Religion: burden of, 99-100; generalized approaches to, 30, 31, 37,
93; as "good," 43, 49, 56, 61, 64,
154-155; Hebrew prophets and,
162-163; and ideology, 178; institutional growth of, 21-23; partic-
ularized understanding of, 31-32,
37, 93; and political life, 53, 119-
120, 129-130; and psychology, 74;
revival of interest in, 17-20, 21 ff.;
and science, 38, 105-106; and social approval, 25, 44; utilitarian
view of, 44-49, 52, 54-55, 56, 57-
58, 74-75, 84-90, 128, 165-166, 167-
169; *see also under* America,
American religion, Folk religion,
Piety, the new
Revivalism, 72, 93 ff.: and church,
108-111; and frontier America,
101-102; futility of, 111-114; and
race question, 170-171; usage of
term, 115; *see also* Graham, Billy
Richardson, Alan, 187
Riesman, David, 18, 36
Russell, Jane, 180

Schlesinger, Arthur M., Jr., 20
Schneider, Herbert W., 27, 38, 39-

40, 41, 61-62, 62-63, 64, 67, 143,
152
Science, and religion; *see under* Re-
ligion
Secularism, 129, 174: and religion,
33-34, 35; and communism, 124
"Sick-souled" outlook, 73, 89, 181
Sin, 55, 97, 112, 117, 126, 147, 163,
172-173, 174
Smith, Adam, 129, 132
Smith, Ronald Gregor, 26, 39
Social gospel: basis of, 176; and
Christian missions, 173; motiva-
tion for, 170, 173-174; and per-
sonal gospel, 169-176; *see also
under* Christian faith
Spencer, Herbert, 87
Spiritual Mobilization, 47-48, 65-66,
124, 128, 139
Steere, Douglas V., 137, 151
Success: and failure, 88-90; as goal,
44-45, 84-88; *see also under* "Cult
of reassurance"

Theology: and ideology, 166; and
idolatry, 166
Thomas, George F., 188
Tillich, Paul, 84, 98-100, 103, 116,
166-167, 188
Trembley, Francis J., 91
Trinity, doctrine of, 108, 185-186

Utopianism, 107, 168-169, 172

Vereide, Abraham, 65

Whitehead, Alfred North, 71, 72
Whyte, William H., Jr., 139-142,
144, 151, 152, 164-165, 172, 187,
188

1779

Date Due